LIBRA

24 SEPTEMBER – 23 OCTOBER

First published in Great Britain 2011
by Mills & Boon, an imprint of Harlequin (UK) Limited,
Eton House, 18-24 Paradise Road, Richmond, Surrey TW9 1SR

Copyright © Dadhichi Toth 2011

ISBN: 978 0 263 89657 2

Design by Jo Yuen Graphic Design
Typeset by KDW DESIGNS

Harlequin (UK) policy is to use papers that are natural, renewable
and recyclable products and made from wood grown in sustainable
forests. The logging and manufacturing processes conform to the
legal environmental regulations of the country of origin.

Printed and bound in Spain
by Blackprint CPI, Barcelona

Dedicated to

The Light of Intuition

Sri V. Krishnaswamy—mentor and friend

With thanks to

Joram and Isaac

Special thanks to

Nyle Cruz for

initial creative layouts and ongoing support

✦ ABOUT DADHICHI ✦

Dadhichi is one of Australia's foremost astrologers and is frequently seen on television and in other media. He has the unique ability to draw from complex astrological theory to provide clear, easily understandable advice and insights for people who want to know what their futures may hold.

In the 26 years that Dadhichi has been practising astrology, face reading and other esoteric studies, he has conducted over 10,000 consultations. His clients include celebrities, political and diplomatic figures, and media and corporate identities from all over the world.

Dadhichi's unique blend of astrology and face reading helps people fulfil their true potential. His extensive experience practising Western astrology is complemented by his research into the theory and practice of Eastern forms of astrology.

Dadhichi has been a guest on many Australian television shows, and several of his political and worldwide forecasts have proved uncannily accurate. He appears regularly on Australian television networks and is a columnist for online and offline Australian publications.

His websites—www.dadhichi.com and www.facereader. com—attract hundreds of thousands of visitors each month, and offer a wide variety of features, helpful information and services.

MESSAGE FROM
❧ DADHICHI ❧

Hello once again and welcome to your 2012 horoscope book!

Can you believe it's already 2012? Time flies by so quickly and now here we are in this fateful year, a time for which several religions of the world—including the Mayans from 3100BC—have predicted some extraordinary events that are supposedly going to affect us all!

Some people are worried there will be a physical cataclysm that will kill millions and millions. Some are of the opinion it is the end of the economic and social models we have lived by for thousands of years. Others seem to believe the Planet Nibiru will whiz by planet Earth and beam up the 144,000 Chosen Ones.

Whatever the opinion, it is an undeniable fact that we are experiencing some remarkable worldwide changes due to global warming (even though that remains a point of contention) and other societal shifts. Scientific knowledge continues to outrun our ability to keep up with it, and time appears to be moving faster and faster.

But my own research has categorically led me to repeat: 'Relax, everyone; it is *not* the end of the world!' There will most certainly be a backlash at some point by Mother Earth at the gross unconsciousness of many of us. There will be ravaging storms, earthquakes and other meteorological phenomena that will shake the Earth, hopefully waking up those of us still in a deep sleep, dreaming, or possibly even sleepwalking. It is time to open our eyes and take responsibility.

If there are any significant global changes I foresee, they are the emergence of wider self-government and the greater Aquarian qualities of the coming New Age. This period is the cusp or changeover between the Age of Pisces, the Fish, and the Age of Aquarius, the Dawn of Higher Mankind.

Astrology, and these small books I write about it, are for the sole purpose of shedding light on our higher selves, alerting us to the need to evolve, step up to the plate, and assume responsibility for our thoughts, words and deeds, individually and collectively. The processes of karma are ripe now as we see the Earth's changes shouting to us about our past mistakes as a civilisation.

I hope you gain some deeper insight into yourself through these writings. For the 2012 series I have extended the topics and focused more on relationships. It is only through having a clear perception of our responsibility towards others that we can live the principles of astrology and karma to reach our own self-actualisation, both as individuals and as a race.

I hope you see the light of truth within yourself and that these words will act as a pointer in your ongoing search.

All the best for 2012.

Your Astrologer,

www.dadhichi.com
dadhichitoth@gmail.com
Tel: +61 (0) 413 124 809

CONTENTS

❦ CONTENTS ❦

❧ CONTENTS ❧
CONTINUED

2012: Monthly and Daily Predictions

2012: Astronumerology

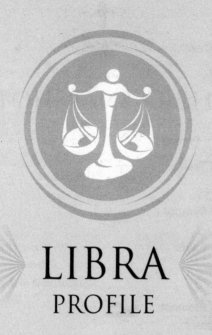

LIBRA
PROFILE

HE WHO LETS TIME RULE HIM WILL
LIVE THE LIFE OF A SLAVE.

John Arthorne

✻ LIBRA SNAPSHOT ✻

Key Life Phrase		I Balance
Zodiac Totem		The Scales
Zodiac Symbol		♎
Zodiac Facts		Seventh sign of the zodiac; moveable, barren, masculine and dry
Zodiac Element		Air
Key Characteristics		Refined, social, artistic, vacillating, intellectual, communicative, concerned with relationships
Compatible Star Signs		Gemini, Aquarius, Leo and Sagittarius
Mismatched Signs		Aries, Capricorn, Cancer and Taurus

Ruling Planet		Venus
Love Planets		Saturn and Uranus
Finance Planets		Sun, Mars and Pluto
Speculation Planets		Saturn and Uranus
Career Planets		Moon, Jupiter and Neptune
Spiritual and Karmic Planets		Mercury, Saturn and Uranus
Friendship Planet		Sun
Destiny Planets		Saturn and Uranus
Famous Librans		Usher, Will Smith, Zac Efron, Matt Damon, Hugh Jackman, Sting, Bruce Springsteen, Mario Lopez, Simon Cowell, John Lennon, Clive Owen, Gwyneth Paltrow, Naomi Watts, Christina Milian, Avril Lavigne, Gwen Stefani, Kate Winslet, Susan Sarandon, Neve Campbell, Catherine Zeta-Jones, Sharon Osbourne and Monica Bellucci

Lucky Numbers and Significant Years	5, 6, 8, 14, 15, 17, 23, 24, 26, 32, 33, 35, 41, 42, 44, 50, 51, 53, 60, 61, 69, 77, 78, 80 and 87
Lucky Gems	Clear quartz, diamond, white coral and zircon
Lucky Fragrances	Rose, geranium, clary sage, frankincense and tangerine
Affirmation/ Mantra	I am harmonious in body, mind and spirit
Lucky Days	Wednesday, Friday and Saturday

✦ LIBRA OVERVIEW ✦

Most people know you as an extremely sociable and fun-loving person, but at the heart of your Libran personality, the desire for popularity—to be loved and cherished—is so deep that few realise how powerfully this need influences everything you do.

In your search to be accepted and loved, you will discover creative and cultural avenues to put you in touch with those people who are going to be instrumental in fulfilling your destiny.

You seek out people who have an intellectual rapport with you. This is due to the fact that your star sign is aligned with the element of air, which has everything to do with the mind, thoughts, ideas and, of course, communication, which is really your forte.

Yes, you love people and a social environment in which you can exchange ideas, but not at the expense of your peace and balance. In the early stages of your life, the Scales of Justice, which represent your star sign, may actually be quite out of whack and imbalanced.

I've met many Librans who struggle with the idea of balance and harmony, and this will be a motivating factor in your relationships and life experiences as well. Finding that perfect equilibrium is the driving force in your character.

Part of what causes the scales to tip to one side or the other is your idealism. You tend to see the world through rose-coloured glasses, especially in your search for true friends and lovers. Unfortunately, this may also inhibit the peace and happiness that you so desperately seek.

You're a gentle person, sharing what you have with those you feel are worthy of your love. You abhor disharmony, quarrels and any sort of confrontational situation that can upset your peace of mind, and are therefore quick to step away from such circumstances.

You love the finer things in life; anything that seems brutish, low class or abrasive to your refined sense of culture will be dismissed very quickly. In friendships, you are sometimes quick to put others on a pedestal and will be severely disappointed if you realise they possess any Neanderthal traits.

In life, as with anyone else, you will need to make some tough decisions from time to time. If there's anything that could be considered a significant fault with Librans, it is their indecisiveness in such moments. You hate to make a mistake. You therefore go over every possible scenario to make sure your conclusions are correct.

Attractive Libra!

You're attractive, tactful and extremely popular, so you mustn't worry about whether or not people accept you. Simply continue to be yourself, and the rest will fall into place.

If you are a Libran who lacks self-esteem, self-assurance or confidence, you will probably rely a great deal on what your friends and family members have to say about your decisions. You could spend considerable time seeking second- and third-party opinions because you don't trust your own ability to make the right choice.

I suggest that you get considerable practice in this area, to start a life of true independence and freedom. This is the one area that will provide you with the peace, happiness and balance you are hoping to find.

LIBRA'S ARTISTIC FLAIR

Beauty and anything artistic attracts you. If the people you are with have no concern for or interest in these areas, it will be very hard for you to maintain an ongoing relationship with them.

You are the consummate mediator. I'm not only talking in a business sense, but of your overall ability to see both sides of a story. In your family life and social group, you will always be called upon to help resolve disputes because of your impartial approach.

You always look absolutely fabulous, there's no doubt about it. Venus has blessed you with the ability to present the best side of yourself to the world, even when the chips are down. Everywhere you go, heads turn, and you don't even have to work at it. Your charm has just always been there.

If you take that charm and add a smattering of confidence, you will see why Libra is regarded as a lucky sign. People want to help you because you are so cheerful and balanced. Over time, you will attract plenty of friends, well-wishers and even financial patrons, who are more than willing to give you a hand.

However, at times, this may also create difficult situations for you. For example, when trying not to be partial to one friend over another, you can be perceived as lacking decisiveness. Once again, you need to have balance!

❋ LIBRA CUSPS ❋

ARE YOU A CUSP BABY?

Being born on the changeover of two star signs means you have the qualities of both. Sometimes you don't know whether you're Arthur or Martha, as they say! Some of my clients can't quite figure out if they are indeed their own star sign, or the one before, or after. This is to be expected because being born on the borderline means you take on aspects of both. The following outlines give an overview of the subtle effects of these cusp dates and how they affect your personality quite significantly.

Libra-Virgo Cusp

The junction point of two star signs is called the cusp. This is the changeover period where those who are born—in your case, between the 21st and the 29th of September—exhibit some of the characteristics of the native star sign, Libra, and some of the previous sign, Virgo.

The combined influence of the two ruling planets—that is, Venus, the ruler of Libra, and Mercury, the ruler of Virgo—endows you with a very quick and analytical mind. You have an extended awareness, and can apply this to practical matters as well as spiritual insights.

Because you are such a rational person, you take on the critical aspects of Virgo, and can sometimes be extremely difficult to deal with as a result. Your mind is in a hyperactive mode much of the time, and this can tire you out as well as get people offside.

An important point I should make is that with Virgo being the sign of health, and Libra being the sign of sociability, one may affect the other. Living life too hard on the razor's edge is not a good thing for you to do. If you are as aware as I have indicated, then any imbalance will make sense to you, and you'll know you're not living in harmony with what nature has intended.

EMOTION AND INTELLECT

You have a mixture of emotion and mentality, and, at times, you oscillate between the two. You try to make decisions with your feelings and analyse relationships with your mind. Don't you think this is back to front, Libra?

Your body signals will be clearly pronounced and you should listen to what they tell you. Try to keep balance in mind. Don't let the critical side of Virgo overtake your sensibilities, and be gentle on yourself as well—Virgos can be their own worst critics. Love yourself, Libra!

Libra-Scorpio Cusp

The Libra-Scorpio cusp is an intense and passionate one. If you are born between the 19th and the 23th of October, you'll have strong elements of Scorpio influencing your personality.

This is an exciting combination, endowing you with both social graces and intense sexual magnetism. Those born on this cusp are probably some of the most sexually switched-on individuals in the zodiac.

You can easily persuade others to do whatever you want them to, but particularly in the bedroom. This combination makes you a conqueror of romantic partners. However, being born on this cusp means you may have troubles with commitment. For this reason, you need to delve into your past to see what elements of your upbringing might have influenced you and may be working against your best interests.

Although you are overly critical, this usually comes from a deep level of devotion to your friends and family, and often people don't see this. Try to be softer in the way you handle the ones you love. Your desire to push people to bring out their best may backfire and cause you many troubles.

You have a wonderful sense of intuition, and your judgement is profoundly well developed. You use both of these attributes to come up with conclusions that bedazzle others. People wonder how you come up with the ideas that you have—there is an element of mental brilliance associated with births during this time of the year.

There's a great impulsiveness in your nature, which means you need to be careful about being overly self-indulgent or developing compulsions that are hard to overcome. Laziness, too, which is not normally evident in the Scorpio, could sneak into your personality, so always fight the urge to lay back and become a couch potato.

Overall, this cuspal influence is excellent, because eventually it brings peace and harmony to your life. This is the result of the Scorpionic determination to achieve what it is you so desperately desire in life.

LIBRA CELEBRITIES

FAMOUS MALE:
WILL SMITH

World-famous actor Will Smith is a Libran, just like you. Will is the second of four children. He is of both African American and Native American descent, and grew up in a middle-class area in West Philadelphia.

The artistic Venus obviously had a part to play in his first love, which was music. He performed as a DJ, and then became well known as the Fresh Prince when his popularity took off.

He eventually moved into movies. Once again, the Libran talent for communicating ideas in the visual medium of film took him to an even greater level of success. Some of his screen appearances include *The Fresh Prince of Bel-Air* in 1990, *Six Degrees of Separation* in 1993, and the action picture *Bad Boys* in 1995. *Independence Day*, in 1996, was a blockbuster hit and, of course, several subsequent movies, including *Hancock*, have helped him make a permanent mark on the industry, and the hearts of millions of fans worldwide.

Librans are famous for their love of relationships, and their ideal of marriage and family life is no different. I guess Will's following quote sums up this fact: 'I really believe that a man and a woman together, raising a family, is the purest form of happiness we can experience.'

WILL'S LANGUAGE SKILLS

Will speaks fluent Spanish, indicative of yet another Libran talent: languages. He is the first hip hop artist to be nominated for an Academy Award.

FAMOUS FEMALE:
NAOMI WATTS

Although Australians claim her as their own Hollywood star, Naomi Watts was, in fact, born in Shoreham, England, and then yes, was raised in Australia.

Naomi eventually moved to Hollywood and started working regularly, but initially in small roles that she wasn't particularly happy about.

Her big break arrived when she auditioned for *Mulholland Drive* in 2001. She performed so well that she captured the attention of some of the powerbrokers in Hollywood. She is now a leading lady, and enjoys a great reputation with some classic movies to her name, such as the remake of *The Ring* in 2002, *21 Grams* in 2003, and the blockbuster hit by director Peter Jackson, *King Kong*, in 2005.

Another little-known fact is that she's best friends with Australia's other leading lady, Nicole Kidman. She's also a vegetarian. Many Librans are sensitive to the plight of animals and, along with trying to foster better health for themselves, are pacifists who dislike seeing any sort of suffering inflicted on other beings.

NAOMI'S SUCCESS

In 2002 People *magazine nominated her*
as one of its '50 Most Beautiful People'. She's
also been voted one of the sexiest ladies alive
in magazines such as Empire, FHM *and*
Entertainment Weekly.

I love the following quote of Naomi's, because it captures what is at the heart of the Libran ideal: 'You have to make peace with yourself. The key is to find harmony in what you have.' This indeed reflects the great balancing act that many Librans have to contend with. Like Naomi, it is essential that you look to yourself first, especially if you're finding imbalance in your life. By doing so, you'll find the balance that you're looking for.

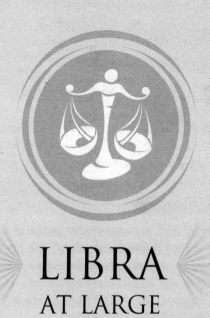

LIBRA
AT LARGE

WE WERE GIVEN TWO HANDS TO
HOLD, TWO LEGS TO WALK, TWO
EYES TO SEE, TWO EARS TO LISTEN.
BUT WHY ONLY ONE HEART?
BECAUSE THE OTHER WAS GIVEN TO
SOMEONE ELSE, FOR US TO FIND.

Anonymous

❧ LIBRA MAN ❧

The Libran man is pretty much unrivalled for charm when it comes to the zodiac signs. The planet Venus is the ruler of Libra and, being feminine in nature, gives men of this sign a natural resonance with women and people in general. As with females born under Libra, the men of the Scales love to socialise.

For the most part, Venus will provide the Libran man with an attractive body and face. Along with physical attractiveness, your personality is enticing and, once others get a taste for it, is also quite addictive. You love this, but you must always be prepared to study others' motives, because often you are simply used for your fun value rather than people truly wanting to understand you.

As mentioned in the introduction, men of this sign hate to confront serious problems, and run for cover when deep and meaningful discussions lead to arguments. The one thing you need to know about the Libran man is that they are happy to talk, but if you start shouting, abusing them or distracting yourself from the topic at hand, they will disappear very quickly, indeed.

A Libran man possesses a great deal of courtesy and gentleness, but it's also true that he's constantly on the lookout for appropriate partners. Because of the quality of air ruling the Libran male, he has a high degree of intelligence, but is restless by nature. This restlessness is also attributed to another facet of the Libra star sign, which is that it is a cardinal or moveable sign. This moving quality is deeply connected to the element of air, which is everywhere, invisible and hard to pin down. I think this best describes the Libran male.

The quality of air, apart from bestowing intelligence upon its owner, makes you, the Libran man, partial to jokes, humour and stimulating discussions about politics, religion and, most importantly, human nature and relationships.

You have a particularly sharp sense of humour and tend to be very witty, and you bring these qualities to any debate or argument in which you can take part. Just remember to listen as well. Don't jump the gun— wait until other people have had their say before you pronounce judgement.

You have a particularly strong sense of relationships. You may find this in either your business or personal life, but you will find it. Relationships are the underlying motivation of a Libra.

A Libran man doesn't shy away from independent activity, but, really, being alone is not easy for you. You are a people person: you like to be with others and share your mind and heart in social settings.

You have great social skills with small groups of people, but you don't enjoy holding centre stage with big groups. You are likely to be well-read and up to date with current affairs.

You enjoy having a great time, and in some ways are an entertainer, especially when it comes to relating stories of your life to others. You're passionate about the way you do this, and people admire your ability to convey your feelings so openly and warmly.

Although I've said that you're the type of person who enjoys being with the opposite sex, when you choose a partner, you like to look after them and share everything you posses with them. Family life is, therefore, a very important element of your future happiness.

Part of your personality—and one of your most notable attributes—is your constant search to understand the human condition. You're fully aware of the plight of people, the injustices of life, and the spiritual and philosophical anomalies that are a part of life. Many of you born under this sign are particularly analytical, and seek answers beyond the realm of this world.

Philosophy gives you an insight into the probable causes of these issues, and the fact that you take such a deep interest in these topics means you need to surround yourself with people of a similar temperament.

Sexy Libra

He's a sexy individual and likes to test the waters (as often as possible) to make sure his attractiveness and powers of seduction are still intact, even in his later years. But more about this in the following segment on Libran sexuality and love.

You are particularly fussy about the kind of people you want in your life. You need them to be sympathetic to the human condition and your interest in it as well. By making friends with people of the same calibre, you will instinctively sidestep boredom, knowing that conversation will continually stimulate you and help you grow as a human being.

LIBRA WOMAN

LIBRA WOMAN: SNAPSHOT

Sexy

Sociable

Impartial

Indecisive

Chatty

I wouldn't be incorrect in assuming that you're proud to be a Libran woman, born under the sign of the Scales, because you love the idea that your totem depicts your desire for balance, poise, grace and a love of life. Right?

You have the wonderful skill of being diplomatic and tactful, even when you're drawn into a situation that would leave most people scratching their heads. When friends are in conflict, you're able to quickly cut through the BS and get to a solution that is satisfactory to all concerned. For this reason, people lean on you a little more than they should, but because you have a humanitarian nature, you are happy to take the time, sacrificing your own needs to help others.

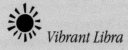

Vibrant Libra

The first impression people will have of you is the vibrant and vivacious energy you carry around even in times of difficulty. You have a bright and effervescent personality that captivates others immediately. Your intelligence is an added benefit that people also respect. So, not only do you attract people's eyes with your good looks and charm, but you just as easily attract their minds and intellect through your witty conversation and broad-mindedness.

You pride yourself on your refined tastes—in your dress sense, in your personal hygiene, in the way you furnish your house and in the environment in which you live— but also in terms of your level of communication and the standards you set for yourself.

You hate lowering yourself to the lowest common denominator. You keep your standards high, and don't belittle yourself by getting involved with people who could sully your name. Integrity is paramount in your life.

Mostly, the Libran woman is creatively concerned with finding the right mate, living up to her ideal of love, and being truly happy in a romantic sense. You'll do anything to maintain the peace and cordiality of a relationship, which is why many of you get involved with your partners' businesses and lives. You're there to help them and act as a cornerstone of their success.

You have a tactful nature, and are quite shrewd in the way you deal with others. Behind your charming, convivial personality is mind constantly ticking over and analysing others. This is why many Libran women become excellent businesspeople and are successful in their chosen lines of work. Your diplomatic mind helps you mix perfectly with all sorts of people because you don't look down on others, even if they are of a lower class. (This doesn't mean you adopt their lowly ways, however.)

You like to entertain, and will create a social atmosphere in your home. People find you an extraordinarily wonderful person to be around, which is why they value your friendship.

While balance is the key word for your star sign, you will, at different times of your life, struggle to balance family with your personal or social needs. You need to dedicate time to this before it spirals out of control. You should keep track of your emotions, balance them, and not rely too much on what other people say. Your hyper-sensitive nature often takes statements too personally. Yes, you're intellectual, but you can sometimes over-react. Why not rely more heavily on your intuition, of which you have oodles?

Try to not rely too much on others for your own happiness. When it comes to seeking the perfect partner, you may end up creating a revolving door of suitors who are unreliable and totally incompatible with you. Play the field but don't surrender your high standards for anyone.

❧ LIBRA CHILD ❧

I only hope that, as the parent of a Libran child, you have an intense interest in communication. If you don't, you'll soon learn to develop the art of conversing and listening.

First and foremost, your little Libran offspring is curious and intellectually activated from the moment he or she is born. This can be extremely demanding, but, nevertheless, you'll need to make time to foster this particular character trait in your child.

The second essential thing for rearing a Libran child is to create a peaceful and harmonious domestic atmosphere. It's a shame to see broken homes have an effect on children of any star sign, but I emphasise this here because of the terrible impact they can have on a child born under the sign of the Scales. If you are going through a separation or divorce, pay special attention to your Libran child's needs, and try to give them a sense that the transition will be seamless. This will help avoid any emotional confusion and upsets, and reduce the stress levels on them under these circumstances.

Your Libran child is a wonderful social being: outgoing, and always trying to foster peace and happiness among their peers. Sometimes, in an effort to make friends, you'll notice that he or she may actually try a little too hard. You need to teach them to relax and accept the fact that who they are, as they are, is sufficient, and they needn't try to be anything other than themselves. As a result, they will naturally attract the right people at the right time.

If you are a busy working mother or father, it's important not to leave your Libran child alone. They hate emptiness, and having no one around to communicate with. If you can't be there, try to organise a babysitter or a friend to keep them company. Of course, I'm not talking only about the young Libran child, but also those who are grown up and more self-sufficient. They, too, need friends, so keep that in mind.

Games and sport will offer them a perfect outlet for their imaginative and clever energies, and help to ground them as well. Strategic games like tennis and soccer, as well as gymnastics, dance and the other creative arts, are the sort of activities that will help direct their energies in the most appropriate ways.

Sometimes, if you're insensitive and say something casually, your Libran child may over-react and take it extremely personally. If they are sulking, it's important to quickly correct that behaviour—go back over your statements and clarifying them so you can explain what was really intended.

Being extremely sensitive to what people say or do, you need to teach your Libra the art of developing a slightly thicker skin, to be more able to deal with the world as they grow older.

At school, the Libran child should do extremely well, particularly in subjects such as art and culture, as well as literature. You should include these in their educational regime to help them develop.

Intelligent Libra

Idle hands are the devil's playground and this is very much the case with Libran children. Because of their highly developed intellectual abilities, it's imperative for you to provide them with ample activities to occupy their brains and hands. They're quite reasonable, and do well in anything of a studious nature.

❈ LIBRA LOVER ❈

Being ruled by Venus is your claim to being one of the most loveable and loving signs of the zodiac. It's as if you instinctively understand what love is, and that the concept of romance is something you are aware of from the point of childhood itself.

The principal attribute that makes you so loveable is your natural inclination to appreciate and admire the person you love. However, for this person, being in that position is not always easy. You have very high standards when it comes to choosing the one to whom you'll give your heart. It's probably for this reason that many Librans, and in particular the males, play the field and explore the possibilities that are available to them.

 Decisions, Decisions

If you involve yourself in many liaisons for the purpose of experience, you might, as I've also found with some Librans, come to the point where the decision between two or more lovers is a reality. The fact that you have the Scales of Justice ruling you means that you oscillate in your choices, and could find it immensely difficult to draw a conclusion.

Your standards, as I've said, are extremely high. This makes it hard for the person who loves you, but also for you, yourself, to accept that it will be impossible for anyone to ever measure up. The reverse of this is that you sometimes put people on such high pedestals that when they fall off, it's hard for you to believe they are, after all, only human.

Your ideals relate to love itself, and everything subsequent to it, such as family life, a good partner, and children. You want to build a comfortable environment for yourself and the ones you love.

Although you love your family and give your all to them, there is still a part of you that needs its own space, independence and the option to meet and interact with many different people. Because of this, your choice of partners is very important—they will need to allow you that space without any possessiveness or jealousy. Under no circumstances can you handle being put in a corner with your hands tied, with no possibility of exploring your social and intellectual worlds. That would be a disaster.

Libra's Love Lessons

Your lesson in love is to accept human frailty as part and parcel of human nature. You must, of course, weigh up all sides in your choice of the perfect one before committing yourself to marriage, however.

In your relationships, you want someone who is elegant, intelligent, witty and hardworking. You need someone who has the same passion and energy for life as you. You also like to have someone who can convey their feelings and ideas, so that the interplay of your minds and hearts is unobstructed, and they can develop in unison.

All in all, your capacity for love is great, but your indecision and idealism may, at times, undermine the very thing you hope to achieve. You must learn to relax, accept others for who they are, and enjoy the path of love.

✣ LIBRA FRIEND ✣

In all my years as an astrologer, I've never found a Libra who hasn't been compassionate and unbiased. The totem of the Scales does seem to reflect the balanced view that Librans have when dealing with others.

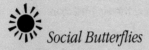

Social Butterflies

The sweet and charming part of a Libran personality is what makes them social butterflies. They're always loved by everyone wherever they go, and they're able to bring zest and interest to any social gathering and event.

You'll find Libras are excellent listeners. Although they often have a great story to tell themselves, it's nice to know that someone's actually taking in and considering your viewpoint, and that they can, if you have a problem, give wonderful advice as well.

However, there are times when Libra is so indecisive that their desire to please everyone becomes rather irritating. There are moments when you need an answer now, and it could involve several people. Because Libra doesn't want to hurt anyone's feelings, you may be waiting a while for them to make a firm decision.

Libras don't particularly care from which echelon of society others come, and are able to be friends with people from all cultures and classes. They are genuinely sincere in their desire to connect with the spiritual part of another human being and not necessarily focused on what they have or what they can get from them.

Your Libran friend is exciting and enthusiastic about everything, but most importantly, about other people. Librans are primarily focused on relationships, so it doesn't matter whether it's a relative, a work colleague or a friend, they always do their best to improve their relationships and get along.

One of the main reasons Libras surround themselves with people is because they detest being alone. Perhaps, if you're a Libra reading this, you should try to distinguish between being alone and being lonely. One of my best pieces of advice to many Librans who come to see me is that they learn to develop the most important relationship of all: their relationship with themselves.

Librans also love to look and be their best to others, which makes them very popular. However, fashion can be a problem when they spend hours and hours looking in the mirror, trying to figure out what the best colour combination or fashion statement is.

What Confrontation?

If you're a friend of a Libra and want to get down to the serious business of discussing an issue, you may end up frustrated—Librans, for the most part, avoid conflict like the plague. Naturally, we all want peace, but if you see them walking away before you get the chance to air your grievances, then this can be a problem.

LIBRA ENEMY

I have to laugh as I speak of Libra as an enemy. My first intuition is of a sheep frolicking about in a field, only to discover, on closer scrutiny, that it is a wolf. Yes, a wolf in sheep's clothing does indeed describe some Libran enemies.

They have such a diplomatic front that at times it's hard to tell when you've annoyed them. Part of their make-up is to always be composed and exhibit balance, even though they may be seething at something you've said or done.

To avoid making a Libra an enemy is probably the best place to start because, although they appear to be quite calm and collected on the outside, when they lose their cool, they do it in such a way that they will tear shreds off you. They dispense with histrionics and other low-level tactics, hitting you verbally and intellectually right where it hurts.

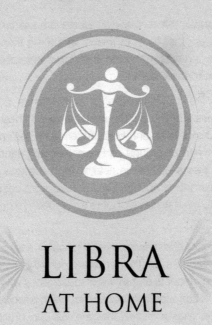

LIBRA
AT HOME

HE IS THE HAPPIEST, BE HE KING OR
PEASANT, WHO FINDS PEACE IN HIS
HOME.

Johann Wolfgang von Goethe

HOME FRONT

Although it's fair to say that Libras are primarily social people, another facet of their character is that they are home loving and inclined to enjoy the comforts of a cosy and comfortable domestic setting.

Librans are known to have expensive tastes, due to the governance of the beauty-inspired Venus. That may be true, but not everyone born under Libra has millions of dollars to throw around on furnishings and exotic tastes in their home. Therefore, let me rephrase and say that elegance and simplicity, even if they don't cost a great deal, are the hallmarks of Libra's approach to decorating and living.

Librans express their creativity, sense of colour balance and design through their choice of furnishings, artworks and other aspects of their living space. They want to relax and feel comfortable in their home, which is why, although they have elegant tastes, they are also very practical.

You, Libra, need to create enough space in your home to entertain, because this is extremely important to keeping you fulfilled as a person. You love to have dinners, invite friends around, and even use part of your house as an area where study and work can take place—anything to keep you in touch with people.

You like a lovely selection of colours, but they always blend in harmoniously without offending one's senses. You use these colours in a creative fashion, and generally the whiter tones—creams, and lighter, sandy or autumn colours—work well for you. Your paintings may possess dashes of red or black as bold contrasts to these subdued colours. You want harmony and softness, but not to the point where it deadens your senses. You still need that excitement which, being part of your nature, is always expressed in your home environment.

You fantasise a lot, so there should be at least one place in your house, such as media room or a meditation room, where you can spend time alone and allow your mind and your imagination to run free.

Some of you reading this may have slightly old-fashioned (and even antique) leanings, and so furniture from earlier eras, along with accessories such as lace, love seats and even wrought iron and glass with intricate designs, would be a wonderful extension of your personality in your home.

Ornamentation is also found in many Libran homes, and this includes art, fragrant candles with elaborate candlesticks, mirrors, and pottery of all shapes, sizes and colours.

The Libran abode is not only comfortable but, in extreme cases, can be an interesting museum to visit.

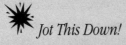 *Jot This Down!*

Libra needs freedom at all times. If you live with a Libra, allow them freedom of movement and creative licence around the home.

KARMA, LUCK AND MEDITATION

Libra, you are endowed with an extraordinary capacity for communication and an understanding of human nature generally. Your past karma sign is Gemini, which explains why you have such an excellent rapport with others.

Mercury rules your past karma and the good fortune you are likely to achieve in this life. Mercury is a quick-moving planet, therefore the fruits of your past actions will usually manifest quickly. It is also a fortunate planet, so generally the results for you are good.

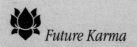

Future Karma

Your future karma and what's likely to happen in your life is ruled by Aquarius and its ruler Uranus. Uranus is progressive, electric and exciting, and therefore Librans usually have an interesting future with many changes that help them cultivate their wisdom.

'I Balance' is your life phrase. Although this is what all Libras aspire to, you'll probably find yourself in circumstances that are often very unbalanced. The onus is on you to work through—in whatever way you can—to find equilibrium in your life and, in particular, in your relationships.

Fridays, Saturdays and Wednesdays are by far your best days for self-development and meditation. Put aside a little time to discover your inner self.

Your Lucky Days

Your luckiest days are Wednesday, Friday and Saturday.

Lucky Numbers

Lucky numbers for Libra include the following. You may wish to experiment with these in lotteries and other games of chance:

6, 15, 24, 33, 42, 51

5, 14, 23, 32, 41, 50

8, 17, 26, 35, 44, 53

Destiny Years

The most significant years in your life are likely to be 6, 15, 24, 33, 42, 51, 78 and 87.

HEALTH, WELLBEING ❧ AND DIET ❧

I've found that the air signs, including Libra, are usually more slender and graceful in their physical appearance. But there are, of course, exceptions to the rule and, being ruled by Venus, women under the sign of the Scales will have a more graceful and curvaceous shape, although they are usually not overweight.

You can enjoy good health, but be careful not to let the influence of Venus cause you to overdo things. A love of pleasure, overeating and excessive drinking, as well as a lack of sleep, may result in physical problems. In a way, Taurus, also ruled by Venus, is a sister sign, and some of the problems associated with it may be visited upon you because of your common rulership. Exercise moderation, Libra.

In terms of problems that are likely to be experienced, the constitutional weakness of Libra is in the kidney and urinary system. Copious amounts of water, less takeaway foods, and foods that aren't overcooked will help bolster your overall wellbeing.

I've also found that many Libras suffer from headaches, including migraines. Becoming overtired, or being unable to sleep from thinking too much, might occur, too. Relaxation, using specific yogic breathing techniques, will help you overcome such concerns.

You should avoid too much milk, ice cream and cheese, and eat lots of fresh fruit and vegetables. Of course, some wholegrains are good for you, but try to avoid overdoing it with starchy foods such as bread, biscuits and other pastries.

The objective of Libra should be to strengthen your kidney function, which, according to Chinese medicine, also feeds life forces to other internal organs.

✤ FINANCE FINESSE ✤

Money turns you on, Libra, because it can afford you the luxuries that are so much a part of your generous nature.

From the point of view of the zodiac, Scorpio, and the ruling planets of Pluto and Mars, have formed a unity over the way you earn money and, to some extent, the way you spend it—although Virgo and the planet Mercury will have more to say about that. You can be frugal when you want to, yet on the other hand, there are times when you recklessly blow all the money you've saved.

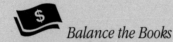

Balance the Books

The safest bet for you, Libra, is to try to balance your finances, because balance, being the operative word for your star sign, should be something that you take to like a duck to water. However, that's not always the case, especially with money.

You like to throw lavish parties and spend big. You like giving and receiving glamourous gifts because of your generosity. But at the end of the day, you also need to look after your future and save in a systematic and logical way.

Try using money wisely, and as a means to an end, rather than as something that you relate to for the sake of impressing others.

LIBRA
AT WORK

PROFESSIONALISM IS KNOWING
HOW TO DO SOMETHING, WHEN TO
DO IT, AND DOING IT.

Frank Tyger

LIBRA CAREER

IDEAL PROFESSIONS

Sales and marketing

Public relations

Human relations

Mediation

Architecture

Interior design

Graphics

There are a few aspects of your Libran nature that make you a sought after worker in any business or endeavour.

Cutting corners is not the way you do things, and when people watch you work, they may be forgiven for mistaking you for a Virgo. There is an aspect of perfection in everything you do. You like to take your time, and don't necessarily want to go back over things if you make mistakes.

Many Libras who aspire to positions of authority find it difficult to make the jump, because they become loyal to their friends and co-workers. If you're in a position to take that leap into a managerial or executive role, you'll either find it difficult to move on or, once you get there, you could experience even greater difficulty in exerting your authority over those who were once your workmates. You need to draw a line in the sand and be more ruthless in the execution of your duties if that's the case.

You're friendly and sociable, and as I've said on several occasions, you work diligently, creatively and persistently to finish a task. But there is another side to you, Libra, and this can get you into trouble. You're so friendly and sociable that often you get distracted and forget yourself. Keep an eye on the time, and don't overdo your socialising, especially at the expense of your employer.

....

PEOPLE PERSON LIBRA

Libra being the public-relations zone of the zodiac means you have a natural affinity for people-related fields such as sales, marketing and mediation. These careers give you an opportunity to shine.

....

Just remember to work in an environment that allows you to express your inner self harmoniously, and do work that is meaningful. As a result, you'll surely achieve success and happiness in your working life.

 Jupiter and Neptune

Your workplace planets are Jupiter and Neptune. What does this mean to you professionally? You are idealistic, and love a happy-go-lucky atmosphere in which to work. Work is important to you, and is a means of personal growth as well as earning money.

Fairness and honesty are key to your work ethic, and this is obvious to anyone who works with you. Unfortunately, others may take advantage of you, and you need to be aware that, at times, your honesty can work against your best interests.

 The Moon

Libra's career ruler is the Moon. Because the Moon is so changeable, the work you do needs variety. Without it, you might lack concentration. Focus on the work at hand, and don't let dissatisfaction creep into your professional activities.

Your indecision has come up quite a bit in this year's reading, and it's essential for me to say that it's likewise going to present problems in being a more ruthless businessman or woman.

At times, you prefer to go easy on clients who are not punctual or who are themselves indecisive. Do your business in a gentle but firm manner, and try not to mix your professional and personal activities too much.

❋ LIBRA BOSS ❋

You probably wonder how it's possible for a Libran boss to do so much with so little time. For those who work for an employer born under the sign of the Scales, I'll tell you upfront that they are the consummate multi-taskers of the zodiac. Along with Gemini, they are capable of successfully managing many things at once.

Your Libran boss is intelligent, able to sell ice to the Eskimos, and loves the fact that they can impress and pursue anyone with whom they come into contact.

If problems occur in your workplace, you'll notice that your Libran boss is genuinely impartial. That trait makes it hard for those who want to ingratiate themselves and get special favours in return.

If decisions need to be made, your Libran boss will *eventually* make up his or her mind, but don't hold your breath. Their indecision—or should I say, their desire to make the right decision—can take much longer than most other people.

The air signs, such as Libra, causes these natives to be predominately intellectual by nature. Analysing, collating and poring over notes and to-do lists will be part of your boss's make-up. This both helps and hinders them in their decision-making, which, as I've just mentioned, can be quite an uphill battle. But when they do come to a conclusion, it will be fair, balanced and usually right.

Believe it or not, your Libran boss is quite progressive, having Aquarius as the other air sign in the zodiac triangle. This makes their minds quick and forward-thinking and their tastes eclectic. You're quite blessed if you have a boss born under the sign of the Scales.

LIBRA EMPLOYEE

 Dapper Employee

If you employ a Libra, you can rest assured you'll never need to take them to task for looking bad, dressing scrappily or forgetting to polish their shoes. Yes, a Libra employee can dress immaculately, adding more power to their already charming and enticing personality. This will serve to promote your company, foster goodwill with clients, and make you feel as if you have a class act representing your interests.

A Libran employee is sensitive, intelligent and capable of handling many tasks at once. But being a moveable sign of the zodiac, they need variety, autonomy and a creative sense of independence to function at their best.

They have a great logical mind, and should, in particular, be employed to resolve problems, negotiate deals and mediate on a variety of different issues. This is the way you'll extract the best from a Libran employee.

As a Libra reading this, you probably identify with many of these points. An additional item (that I think hits the nail on the head, too) is just how important peace and tranquillity in the workplace is for you. You love to have the right ambience in your environment to perfect your work. And, being a creative person, you don't like that process interfered with too much. On the one hand, your seclusion allows you to produce wonderful, unrivalled work; on the other, it can irritate those who need to interrupt you to tell you this, that or the other.

In your creative intensity you may inadvertently offend others, dismissing them too quickly. If balance is your middle name, then you should apply it to your work and the way you deal with co-workers. Balance your creative needs with the needs of the group.

If you're working with people who are respectful, who can air their grievances without shouting, and who can respect you for your creative and intellectual skills, then you'll reach the top of your game.

NO CORNER OF THE OFFICE, THANKS

Employers would be making a terrible mistake if they put you in a corner somewhere and gave you a drone's job such as filing or something else that has little mental stimulation for you.

PROFESSIONAL RELATIONSHIPS: ❀ BEST AND WORST ❀

BEST PAIRING: LIBRA AND LIBRA

There is every possibility that a relationship with your star twin, Libra, could work, because you each reflect the same values.

However, in business, it is essential there is clarity over who is going to do what roles, and when it comes down to it, decision making is not exactly your forte, Libra.

With your endless searches to draw conclusions, you will need to eliminate the to-ing and fro-ing that confronts you. This will impact upon your business, and ultimately cause problems between you.

Being social creatures, the two of you will become great friends, and doing business will quite likely be a lot of fun. But business is business, and you should both commit to the ideal of keeping business and pleasure distinctly separate— at least until you both feel confident that your venture is going to be successful and has sufficient cash flow.

Doing too many things at once is one of the dangers that could impact on the relationship. Running around and always trying to present your best face could distract you from the more routine, humdrum essentials of business. Perhaps you should take turns, because someone always needs to be in the driver's seat, so to speak.

Your hectic business lives may also be hit with some interference, because your social agendas could cramp your business style. All these things need to be carefully addressed before you firmly commit to each other.

Once you have established a plan you're both happy with, you will feel comfortable in your individual and collective roles. From this position, you will have the perfect environment in which to work, and have easygoing but productive surroundings.

WORST PAIRING:
LIBRA AND CANCER

You should steer clear of Cancerians as business partners, even though, in the astrological scheme, Cancer falls in your career sector of the zodiac. Let me explain why.

You may well be attracted to Cancer, because your first encounter with them makes you feel as if they are strong, tough, seasoned business people and yes, many of them are. However, you may have overlooked the fact that the tough exterior of Cancer is a shield, a method by which they hide their deep and sensitive feelings. Once you get to know them a little better, you'll spy the cracks in their shells and witness the changeability and moodiness that is deeply ingrained in the Cancerian psyche.

Their mood swings, along with your indecisiveness, can create major trauma, and you are both prone to conflict and disruption as a result.

You are an air sign, which means you use reasonable and logical approaches to solving problems, both of a business and personal nature. Your Cancerian partner prefers to act on an intuitive platform however, and to you this doesn't make sense. You need to know that the functioning of your business is rational, logical and contained within a workable set of parameters. Cancer's intuitive hunches may sometimes be correct but it makes you feel very uncomfortable.

Your Cancerian partner is caring and giving by nature, so they will work to serve you to their best ability. This is something you do like about them, but you'll still feel as if the energy with which they mother everyone would better utilised in growing the business, connecting with clients and dealing with professionals outside your commercial concern.

All in all, this is a pretty terrible combination and one that should be approached with due caution on your part.

LIBRA
IN LOVE

YOU KNOW YOU'RE IN LOVE WHEN
YOU CAN'T FALL ASLEEP BECAUSE
REALITY IS FINALLY BETTER THAN
YOUR DREAMS.

Dr. Seuss

ROMANTIC
❧ COMPATIBILITY ❧

How compatible are you with your current partner, lover or friend? Did you know that astrology can reveal a whole new level of understanding between people, simply by looking at their star sign and that of their partner? I'd like to share some special insights that will help you better appreciate your strengths and challenges using Sun sign compatibility.

The Sun reflects your drive, willpower and personality. The essential qualities of two star signs blend like two pure colours that produce an entirely new colour. Relationships, similarly, produce their own emotional colours when two people interact. The following section is a general guide to your romantic prospects with others and how, by knowing the astrological 'colour' of each other, the art of love can help you create a masterpiece.

Each of the twelve star signs has a greater or lesser affinity with the others. The two quick-reference tables will show you who's hot and who's not as far as your relationships are concerned.

The Star Sign Compatibility table rates your chance as a percentage of general compatibility, while the Horoscope Compatibility table summarises the reasons why. The results of each star sign combination are also listed.

When reading I ask you to remember that no two star signs are ever *totally* incompatible. With effort and compromise, even the most difficult astrological matches can work. Don't close your mind to the full range of life's possibilities! Learning about each other and ourselves is the most important facet of astrology.

Good luck in your search for love, and may the stars shine upon you in 2012!

STAR SIGN COMPATIBILITY
FOR LOVE AND FRIENDSHIP
(PERCENTAGES)

	Aries	Taurus	Gemini	Cancer	Leo	Virgo	Libra	Scorpio	Sagittarius	Capricorn	Aquarius	Pisces
Aries	60	65	65	65	90	45	70	80	90	50	55	65
Taurus	60	70	70	80	70	90	75	85	50	95	80	85
Gemini	70	70	75	60	80	75	90	60	75	50	90	50
Cancer	65	80	60	75	70	75	60	95	55	45	70	90
Leo	90	70	80	70	85	75	65	75	95	45	70	75
Virgo	45	90	75	75	75	70	80	85	70	95	50	70
Libra	70	75	90	60	65	80	80	85	80	85	95	50
Scorpio	80	85	60	95	75	85	85	90	80	65	60	95
Sagittarius	90	50	75	55	95	70	80	85	85	55	60	75
Capricorn	50	95	50	45	45	95	85	65	55	85	70	85
Aquarius	55	80	90	70	70	50	95	60	60	70	80	55
Pisces	65	85	50	90	75	70	50	95	75	85	55	80

In the compatibility table above please note that some compatibilities have seemingly contradictory ratings. Why you ask? Well, remember that no two people experience the relationship in exactly the same way. For one person a relationship may be more advantageous, more supportive than for the other. Sometimes one gains more than the other partner and therefore the compatibility rating will be higher for them.

HOROSCOPE COMPATIBILITY
❁ FOR LIBRA ❁

Libra with		Romance/Sexual
Aries		Opposites often attract, but in your case, they don't
Taurus		Out of sync and needs adjustment; moments of intense pleasure, but generally very different temperaments
Gemini		Marvellous combination—great mental rapport in the bedroom, a playful association
Cancer		Intimacy can be good, but you'll need to rely on Cancer's moods for the right moment

	Friendship		Professional
✔	A good combination and stimulating	✘	Good business partnership if you submit to Aries' dominance
✘	A busy social life, but Taurus is more grounded and home loving, and could be a wet blanket	✔	Taurus has good financial instincts— you can trust them and possibly do well together
✔	Excellent mental rapport and fun times together	✔	Your intellectual connection will bring you success in business
✘	With a little work, you can indeed enjoy peace and harmony with a Cancerian friend	✘	Cancer's imagination is excellent for business but you need more stability than they can offer

Libra with		Romance/Sexual
Leo		Excellent combination, with Leo's fiery nature being fuelled by your warmth and love
Virgo		You'll like exploring each other sexually, but Virgo may be too *hygienic* for your tastes
Libra		A sensitive and loving union, but it blows hot and cold
Scorpio		Dynamic partnership and sexually quite good; may not be a long-term thing, though
Sagittarius		Good combination, fiery in the bedroom and also intimately fulfilling

Friendship		Professional
✔	Once you get to know each other, your common interests will give you both great satisfaction	✔ You gain from your association with Leo; a great financial connection
✘	Virgo demands and expects a high standard, and your best just may not be good enough	✔ Virgo should be the accountant and you the PR person—this arrangement can work
✔	You both love people and each other, you have fun and communicate well	✘ Too much socialising can detract from the job of effectively executing your plans
✔	You are fascinated by Scorpio's deep perception of life; great communication	✔ You can gain from Scorpio—they are hard workers and you have the ability to promote the business
✔	Exciting and fun times; a lot of travel will give you memorable experiences	✘ Too much fun may distract the two of you from serious business, but with discipline, you can be successful

Libra with		Romance/Sexual
Capricorn	💔	Capricorn is slow to rouse, but may give you moments of pleasure
Aquarius	🔥	Electric romance, with inventive and exploratory lovemaking
Pisces	💧	A good spiritual combination for lovemaking, but not altogether your cup of tea physically

	Friendship		Professional
✘	Natural friendships will evolve, but Capricorn may be too serious	✔	Excellent business partner, the rapport between you should bring financial and professional benefits
✔	Natural and friendly connection between you, a zany and exciting rapport	✘	Aquarius is unconventional, so you may need to adapt considerably to make your business alliance work
✘	Mismatched due to the water versus air elements; it could work, but you'll need to be patient	✔	You just have to trust Pisces' intuitive hunches, which are usually correct—trust is essential in this relationship

❦ LIBRA PARTNERSHIPS ❦

 Libra + Aries

Aries is decisive, but you aren't, Libra. If you can hand over much of the decision making to Aries, your relationship with them can work well. The fire and air combination is quite a zesty one that makes for excitement.

 Libra + Taurus

The earthy Taurus will be whipped into a dust storm by your airy quality, Libra. Although your ruling planet, Venus, is a common element, there are too many differences in this relationship to make it one you can count on.

 Libra + Gemini

This is a wonderful combination, and one that will satisfy both of you to the core. Based primarily on your communication, your intimacy quotient is also quite high.

Libra + Cancer

Both of you are feminine signs of the zodiac, and are therefore sensitive to each other's needs. However, you both swing emotionally—to extremes at that—and this creates an unstable scenario for you.

 Libra + Leo

The romantic attraction between the two of you is strong, and you can be good friends as well as socially captivating to your peers. This should be an excellent partnership.

 Libra + Virgo

You are free and easygoing by nature, and love spontaneous action, whereas Virgo tends to prefer a fixed timetable and a logical sequence for things. It may or may not work.

Libra + Libra

The hectic flow of life and social events for the two of you may be distracting. Vow to each other that you will give quality time to the relationship to make it work.

Libra + Scorpio

Scorpio's penetrating mind will fascinate you, and of course, they are the sexiest of the zodiac signs. Great mental and physical interactions create potential for your relationship with them.

Libra + Sagittarius

Sagittarius is frank, straightforward and sometimes a little hard to handle. Their bluntness could irritate your more graceful style of etiquette. Accept them for who they are, and this will be a great relationship.

Libra + Capricorn

Your star signs are quite friendly, but you need to draw the Saturnine Capricorn out of their deep moodiness. This relationship will be slow to start, but will have some potential in the future.

Libra + Aquarius

This is a fun-filled, exciting, and in some ways, unpredictable relationship. You'll be enamoured by the progressive mind of Aquarius, so you can expect some fun albeit tentative times as well.

Libra + Pisces

The two of you are at cross-purposes in this relationship. Pisces is a feeler and you, Libra, are a thinker. You need to bridge the gap between these extremes to create something worthwhile for the two of you.

PLATONIC RELATIONSHIPS: BEST AND WORST

BEST PAIRING: LIBRA AND SAGITTARIUS

By far one of the best—if not *the* best—platonic relationships you can expect is with the fire sign of Sagittarius. The Sagittarian is outgoing, generous, sociable, and very warm when it comes to love affairs.

Although your ruling planets, Venus and Jupiter, respectively, are not particularly friendly, they do bring forth considerable luck when they combine. Therefore, you could be rather fortunate on many levels, particularly in the realm of friendship.

Communication flows easily, and you appreciate the fact that your Sagittarian friend is forthright in their expression. You love the fact that they have a wealth of experience and an intellectual (and even somewhat a philosophical) view of life, which you want to connect with.

The other aspect of Sagittarius that fits so well with you is their love of people. Both of you are sociable characters, and you can find some very interesting similarities between your star signs. Sagittarius is also an adventure seeker, and the idea of exploring the world, meeting new people and inviting new cultures into your lives is something that turns you on.

If you need someone to talk to, Sagittarius is an open person who's prepared to take the time to listen to your issues. Usually, they're so easygoing that you won't feel judged in this respect.

You need to feel confident that a friend will listen to what you have to say, and Sagittarius gives you this assurance, thus making this a really good match.

WORST PAIRING: LIBRA AND ARIES

I thought long and hard about throwing Aries under the bus when it came to your compatibility with them. I'll give you my reasons, even though you're probably scratching your head, wondering why your opposites don't attract.

Libra and Aries are known to be very attracted to each other, and I can cite a few examples from my collection. In fact, the immediate attraction between the Venus-ruled Libra and the Mars-ruled Aries is quite intense. But the reality is that fiery Aries is so decisive and upfront, that they may intimidate you a great deal.

Likewise, your indecision is a turn-off to them, and although you'll try to be civil with each other, the fact of the matter is that there will be considerable tension underpinning the friendship.

You have a more refined form of communication and etiquette, and feel somewhat embarrassed when Aries tries to upstage you or one-up others in conversation. You'd like to see much more balance displayed by your Aries friend, but unfortunately, that may not be happen.

Both of you are sociable and thrive on cordial conversation with a range of people. However, Aries will try to dominate the situation, and always likes to be right.

Interestingly, you will stimulate Aries with your quality of air and, because Aries is a fire sign, they can blaze brightly in your presence. But given time, you'll realise that this is more of a one-way street, and your needs in this relationship may not be fulfilled by your Aries companion.

SEXUAL RELATIONSHIPS: ❁ BEST AND WORST ❁

BEST PAIRING: LIBRA AND AQUARIUS

Hand in glove is usually a pretty perfect fit, which is why I begin the reading for the two of you with this imagery. That's right: Aquarius, being an air sign like yourself, is an excellent match, one that I would consider to be the best for you. Air signs are always intellectual, communicative and full of ideas.

You have a great attraction for the spontaneous and witty character of Aquarius, but on a deeper level, have great admiration for the fact they can think outside the square, and extend their ideas and concepts of social and global reform. Politics, philosophy and religion are some of the topics that interest them, and these serve to open your mind and heart to new ideas.

Being so relaxed on the level of communication is the reason you'll open up so easily to them, which seems like a natural progression towards a sexual relationship together. You like the idea that they are unconventional in the bedroom as well.

Like you, Aquarians tend to play the field to get a feel for what's right for them. Once you meet each other and connect intellectually (and then physically) you'll realise that you may not need to look any further to find fulfilment on an intimate level.

> *Aquarius is an absolutely wonderful fit for you, and*
> *will stimulate your thinking and intellectual ideas to*
> *the max. The feeling will be mutual, with Aquarius*
> *admiring your social and communication skills.*

Commitment may be an issue that you both skirt around for a while. However, once you realise that, on most levels, you're very compatible, you'll both be prepared to accept that this could be a relationship made in heaven. The two of you will never be bored. Finding ways to stimulate each other will become a passion for the two of you. In short, this truly is an excellent relationship that should be pursued.

WORST PAIRING:
LIBRA AND PISCES

There are just so many differences between a Libra and Pisces match that I wonder why the two of you got together in the first place. Your ruling planet of Venus does tend to become exalted in the sign of Pisces, but this may have more to do with an altruistic connection than with physical attraction.

In connecting with a Pisces, you find it difficult to get your head around the way that they respond to others. Of course, you'll love the sensitive, selfless attitude that your Piscean partner exhibits, but you may not feel complete when it comes to sharing ideas and communicating concepts to each other.

At times, you feel completely disconnected from Pisces. Or rather, Pisces appears to be off with the fairies. There are times you'll talk to them and feel as if they haven't heard a word you've said. This is because they are often in a meditative state, contemplating who knows what. This will irritate you because, as a Libra, you need to know that your partner's attention is 100 per cent on you. But that may not always be the case with Pisces.

Pisces is not quite as social as you and can, like its Cancerian water sign cousin, be rather moody, and even temperamental. When it comes to finding out what the problem is, they may not be able to articulate them as easily as you do. That will become very frustrating for you, and can interfere with your desire to please each other physically.

Pisces lives in the realm of feelings, and has intuitive responses to life. This is different to the air sign of Libra, which has more of an intellectual, cerebral approach to life and relationships.

This is a relationship that may attract you initially, but is one that could be considered a booby trap. Keep your wits about you and, at best, maintain cordial relations with your Pisces friend, but tread very carefully if you decide to cross the line into the romantic sphere. It may just not work.

QUIZ:
HAVE YOU FOUND YOUR PERFECT
❋ MATCH? ❋

Do you dare take the following quiz to see just how good a lover you are? Remember, although the truth sometimes hurts, it's the only way to develop your relationship skills.

We are all searching for our soulmate: that idyllic romantic partner who will fulfil our wildest dreams of love and emotional security. Unfortunately, finding true love isn't easy. Sometimes, even when you are in a relationship, you can't help but wonder whether or not your partner is right for you. How can you possibly know?

It's essential to question your relationships and to work on ways that will improve your communication and overall happiness with your partner. It's also a good idea, when meeting someone new, to study their intentions and read between the lines. In the first instance, when your hormones are taking over, it's easy to get carried away and forget some of the basic principles of what makes for a great relationship that is going to endure.

You're probably wondering where to start. Are you in a relationship currently? Are you looking for love, but finding it difficult to choose between two or more people? Are you simply not able to meet someone? Well, there are some basic questions you can ask yourself to discover the truth of just how well suited you and your partner are for each other. If you don't have a partner at the moment, you might like to reflect on your previous relationships to improve your chances next time round.

The following quiz is a serious attempt to take an honest look at yourself and see whether or not your relationships are on track. Don't rush through the questionnaire, but think carefully about your practical day-to-day life and whether or not the relationship you are in genuinely fulfils your needs and the other person's needs. There's no point being in a relationship if you're gaining no satisfaction out of it.

Now, if you aren't completely satisfied with the results you get, don't give up! It's an opportunity for you to work at the relationship and to improve things. But you mustn't let your ego get in the road, because that's not going to get you anywhere.

A Libran lover is idealistic, and desires perfection in love and the attention they receive at all times. They therefore dream of someone special who can love and cherish them forever. Can you find the perfect one?

Here's a checklist for you, Libra, to see if he or she's right for you.

Scoring System:

Yes = 1 point

No = 0 points

❓ Does she or he appreciate and admire you? Do they tell you so?

❓ Does she or he spend a lot of quality time with you?

❓ Does she or he like to hold hands in public?

❓ Is she or he a princess or prince charming, who would do anything for you and for your relationship, without excuses?

❓ Does she or he smile a lot or, even better, is she or he a funny person?

❓ Do they always remember that special date on your calendar, like your anniversary?

❓ Is your partner sweet and thoughtful, giving you surprise gifts just to cheer you up?

❓ Does she or he believe in togetherness, especially on vacation?

❓ Is your partner a gentlewoman/man who respects you and never embarrasses you, either in public or private?

❷ Is she or he patient enough to wait for your decision?

❷ Do they sensitively give you time to dress and apply makeup for special outings?

❷ Do they enjoy plenty of intimacy, and are they daring in the bedroom?

❷ Does she or he give you time to breathe when you need it?

❷ Do they enjoy having night-time talks and cuddle breaks when you need them?

❷ Do they mentally, emotionally, intellectually and spiritually stimulate your being?

❷ Do they feel balanced, contented and in harmony with your relationship?

Have you jotted down your answers honestly? If you're finding it hard to come up with the correct answers, let your intuition help and try not to force them. Of course, there's no point pretending and turning a blind eye to treatment that is less than acceptable, otherwise you're not going to have a realistic appraisal of your prospects with your current love interest. Here are the possible points you can score.

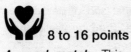

8 to 16 points

A good match. This shows you've obviously done something right, and that the partner you have understands you and is able to reciprocate in just the way you need. But this doesn't mean you should become lazy and not continue working on your relationship. There's always room to improve and make your already excellent relationship even better.

5 to 7 points

Half-hearted prospect. You're going to need to work hard at your relationship, and this will require a close self-examination of just who may be at fault. You know, it takes two to tango and it's more than likely a combination of both your attitudes is what is dragging down your relationship. Systematically go over each of the above questions and try to make a list of where you can improve. I guarantee that your relationship will improve if given some time and sincerity on your part. If, after a genuine effort of working at it, you find things still haven't improved, it may be time for you to rethink your future with this person.

0 to 4 points

On the rocks. I'm sorry to say that this relationship is not founded on a sufficiently strong enough base of mutual respect and understanding. It's likely that the two of you argue a lot, don't see eye to eye or, frankly, have completely different ideas of what sort of lifestyle and emotional needs you each have. The big question here is why are you still with this person?

Again, this requires some honest self-examination to see if there is some inherent insecurity which is causing you to hold on to something that has outgrown its use in your life. Old habits die hard, as they say, and you may also fear letting go of a relationship that you have become accustomed to, even though it doesn't fulfil your needs. Self-honesty is the key here. At certain times in life you may need to make some rather big sacrifices to move on to a new phase, which will then hopefully attract the right sort of partner to you.

2012
YEARLY OVERVIEW

WHATEVER YOUR PAST HAS BEEN,
YOUR FUTURE IS SPOTLESS.

Anonymous

KEY EXPERIENCES

One of the key focuses for most Libras in 2012 will be the issue of money—both in terms of individual earnings and profitability, as well as shared resources, loans and other financial assets.

Saturn, one of your better planets, but nonetheless one that can delay things considerably, makes its entrance into your finance sector in October. Jupiter, on the other hand, continues in your zone of shared resources until June. Matters relating to debts, differences of opinion over the way shared money is spent, etcetera, will be cleared after this point, and make way for Saturn to give you more control over money in the latter part of the year.

On the romantic front, with Venus in your zone of love affairs in January, and then with Mercury, the Sun and Neptune also influencing this area of your life, it's quite likely the first part of the year will be focused on matters of the heart.

ROMANCE AND ❋ FRIENDSHIP ❋

In 2012, anything can and will happen for Libras in their most intimate relationships. The position of Uranus in your sector of marriage and love affairs will see to that.

Because of the presence of the Moon in this area as well, as the year starts, you are likely to shoot from the hip, and not think through some of the relationship decisions you make. Please do balance your heart with your head.

TEST OF MARS AND SATURN

In August, you will feel the full brunt of Mars and Saturn as they try to inflict maximum harm on your personal relationships. If you focus too much on what's wrong with your love life at this time, things will get worse. Ignore these celestial elements, and instead look to what's good about your relationship.

Your ruling planet, Venus, affords you some great opportunities socially and professionally after September. In particular, the transit of Venus through your zone of friendships and life fulfilment throughout all of September and part of October is a lucky omen, and indicates that you'll have the chance to expand your social and influential circles during this period.

Relationships on the Rise

Throughout 2012, there are several key dates when your love life and romantic activities will come to the fore. You can use the following times to take full advantage of what's on offer.

Your love life is in full swing after the 3rd of January, when Venus moves to the fifth sector. Your amorous feelings will continue past the 20th, when the Sun also activates this part of your horoscope.

On the 8th of February, Venus then enters your zone of marriage, and this is when your heart will be all aflutter with thoughts of a stable, long-term love life. If you're married, this could be an excellent time to reconnect with your partner, especially if you haven't had a great deal of time for each other recently.

Once again, playful Mercury moves into the zone of marriage, but its action is a little unpredictable after the 3rd of March, and your communication may need re-evaluating. Promises may be broken, and this could cause confusion in your relationships. Fortunately, Mercury's retrogressive motion continues only until the 4th of April, after which time, things should get back on track.

INTIMATE APRIL

Excitement in your sexual department can be expected from the 19th to the 30th of April. The planets and, in particular, the Sun will bring a new level of intimacy to your most meaningful relationship.

Do be careful of being too strong willed and domineering after the 2nd of August. With Mars impacting heavily on your personal relationships, you are likely to do and say things that are inappropriate and impulsive in nature.

Throughout this period, Mars continues to colour your experiences, and, after the 23rd of August, will further prompt you to say things that may be out of line. Be more diplomatic.

SOCIAL IN SEPTEMBER

Your social life is on the up and up with Venus entering the eleventh zone after the 6th of September. Although you may have problems on the home front, this will be your escape mechanism. Make the most of it.

In October, Venus enters the quiet zone of your horoscope, indicating that you may wish to take time out from the hustle and bustle of city life, and also friends and relations. This is a time for reconnecting with the most important person in your life—yourself! Don't underestimate the importance of this relationship, Libra.

In December, two important celestial events indicate an exciting conclusion to your love life and social activities in 2012. The first is the forward motion of Uranus in your marital sector on the 13th, and the second is Mars's entrance into your zone of love affairs on the 26th. You should prepare yourself for some unexpected twists and turns in your relationships, but these should be reasonably positive. A surprise person may enter your life. In any case, Mars activates your creativity and your sensual nature as well.

WORK AND MONEY

Harness Your Moneymaking Powers

Making money can be summed up in an equation:

$$m \text{ (\$ money)} = e \text{ (energy)} \times t \text{ (time)} \times l \text{ (love)}$$

If one of the above factors is not present—for example, energy or love—you could still make money, but you won't be ideally fulfilled in the process.

It's absolutely essential to understand the universal laws of attraction and success when speaking about money. It is also necessary to understand that when you love what you do, you infuse your work with the qualities of attention, love and perfection.

With these qualities, you endow your work with a sort of electromagnetic appeal: a power that draws people to your work and causes them to appreciate what you do. This, in turn, generates a desire for people to use your services, buy your products and respect you for the great work you perform. This will without a doubt elevate you to higher and higher positions because you will be regarded as someone who exercises great diligence and skill in your actions.

With the presence of Mars in your zone of expenses throughout much of the early part of the year—in fact, up until July—it's likely you may not be frugal or disciplined enough with the way you manage your finances.

My advice to you, Libra, being the sign of the Scales, is to use as much of your balance of power to put a stop to this as you can. If you do, you'll be in a far better position in the second half of the year.

You could expect a turn of events associated with your finances after the 24th of January. The measures you have in place may not work out exactly as planned. Have a Plan B ready.

On the 22nd of February, your finances are in good shape as Mars accentuates your work profile and abilities. Through industriousness and hard work, you can see your financial position getting stronger after this.

Jupiter's influence increases in intensity throughout the year, and by April you'll likely see an increase in your income. Venus also has a hand to play in this, and both of these planets will, in their own way, counterbalance the excesses of Mars that I've just mentioned.

....

JUPITER AND VENUS GET LUCKY

Most astrologers are in agreement that when Jupiter and Venus combine, it's extremely lucky. This year, when they influence your zone of income throughout March and April, you can expect a better position all round in terms of money. Your bank balance will likely increase as well.

....

Venus continues to bless you with some extraordinary opportunities, and throughout May, the combined influence of Saturn and Venus in your zone of contractual arrangements is lucky and, fortunately for Saturn, judicious. You're not likely to lose yourself in the razzle and dazzle of what's being offered, but will be cautious in making the right sort of decision, and getting the appropriate advice.

Whatever legal matters arise this year will not be too much of a concern, as Jupiter brings with it a protective influence after June. Prior to that, however, you mustn't take things for granted.

Your two workplace planets are Jupiter and Neptune. With Neptune in its own place, your vision for better circumstances is broad and quite imaginative. Around the period of July, August and September, there is an improvement in your circumstances, and you're likely to feel more at home and relaxed in the work you are doing. Perhaps some of you Librans have begun on a new path—a new job and environment—and have been feeling your way through. You can start to feel much more confident in your efforts at this time.

With Venus activating your zone of reputation in August and September, this is the period when you can expect great things to happen in your work. Hereafter, most of the year should be smooth sailing, but I must say that an incredibly important transit for you will be that of Saturn into your financial sector after October. This planet reflects on your financial earnings, and the way you deal with money in a completely conservative way. Most Librans will start to deal with their finances in a much more tight-fisted manner at this time.

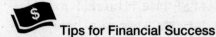

Tips for Financial Success

As mentioned above, you have to be careful to curtail your desire to spend big during the next twelve months. By doing this, you will increase your savings and be able to clearly see that the amount you earn is secondary to the amount you save.

For those of you running independent business concerns, great associations—and even partnerships—can be formed after the 8th of February. You may initially feel as if things are moving too quickly, but the combined influence of Venus and Uranus will bring you good fortune.

Other key times to make hay while the Sun shines include: the direct-movement period of Mercury after the 4th of April; Jupiter's kind aspect to your work zone on the 19th of April, where you can secure the appropriate loans you need for any work you're conducting; and Mercury's entrance into your zone of banking and shared resources on the 9th of May.

These transits herald a new period where you can become far more independent in your working life, and achieve the financial goals you've set for yourself.

ECLIPSE HIGHLIGHT

*The eclipse on the 14th of November occurs in your
zone of finance, and influences your shared resources.
Things could reach a climax at this point, and you
should continue to be vigilant. Get expert advice if you
are not clear on things.*

Profits are up after the 22nd of July, with the Sun moving through your zone of increased business income, but be careful after the 23rd of August, with Mars's entry into your zone of income. Quick profits sometimes lead us to believe, with a false sense of security, that we have more than we actually do. Continue to keep a tight rein on your spending.

 Career Moves and Promotions

One of your key strengths as a Libra is your ability to schmooze and persuade others in whichever direction you choose. In 2012, I see from your horoscope that Venus will continue not only to allow you to enjoy yourself socially, but to use this ability in your search for promotions and enhanced business opportunities.

On the 14th of January, and also the 28th, Venus brings with it a social situation that may be key to furthering your business and professional prospects. Be alert to the signals at that time.

On the 22nd and the 23rd of February, Mars, Venus and Mercury combine their influence to give you excellent communication skills. You may feel uncomfortable in yourself at this time, but it is a good moment to ask your boss for either a pay rise, or that position you've been dreaming of.

In March, there are two key dates I would ask you to note in your diary. They are the 7th and the 21st. On these occasions, the Sun enhances your professional reputation, and on the 21st, Venus kicks in to lend some gracious support.

On the 19th of April, Jupiter, from its position in your area of banking and career, once again offers you a chance for promotion.

You're activated, driven and possibly a little too hardnosed after the 7th of June, but this is precisely what you need to be if you're in a competitive situation and want that job! Mercury enters your zone of professional uplifting on the 7th, and accentuates this fact from the 17th. Communicate your desire for improved circumstances at this time.

NEGOTIATION TIME

Important dates you should note are the 21st of June and the 25th of August, and an important interval is the period from the 5th to the 18th of October. These are all excellent opportunities for you to move forward professionally.

At the end of the year, the 14th of November and the 6th of December once again demand that you put your hand up if you're after a new role. You'll be successful at these times.

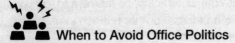
When to Avoid Office Politics

Office politics seem to be part and parcel of work these days, so it's good to know when antagonistic, stressful days are going to ruffle your feathers.

The year kicks off on a temperamental tone, as far as work is concerned, due to the fact that Mars is in the hidden part of your horoscope. What this means for you is that others may be secretly undermining you, and trying to take advantage of you in the workplace. You need to be alert to this, Libra.

Things can intensify in your workplace around the 24th of January. It will be hard for you to bite your tongue, but you must if you are to keep the peace.

Around the 6th of April, the Sun challenges you in your professional life, and you may even be at odds with your employer at this time. It could appear that the whole office is against your ideas, and up until the 10th, you may experience some power plays in your workplace.

Communications may be muddled throughout May, and as early as the 1st, be sure to put your thoughts in writing so there's no ambiguity for your co-workers.

Once again, around the 17th of June, Mercury opposes some of your plans, and what you present to others may be contested, not because of its merits or otherwise, but because someone simply has it in for you. Don't be fazed by this. Stick to your guns.

The retrogression of Mercury is a problem for you around the 15th of July. Don't sign any papers or give your agreement to someone who is pushing you beyond your comfort level.

Around the 18th of October, you have an opportunity for promotion, as was mentioned earlier, but you could find your efforts being utilised by someone vehemently opposed to your success. You might have to fight fire with fire at this time.

Conflicts are likely around the 9th of December, with Mars in a hard right angle to your sign of Libra. Please curb your desire to kill others at this time! It's against the law.

HEALTH, BEAUTY AND
LIFESTYLE

 Venus Calendar for Beauty

You are fortunate in that, like your sister sign of Taurus, you are ruled by Venus, the planet of beauty. Its motion in the heavens is particularly important to your feeling of wellbeing and your attractiveness in 2012.

During 2012, there are some key times when you can avail yourself of the beautiful and uplifting energies of Venus.

When Venus conjoins the sign of Aries, it will shine its gracious light on your Sun sign—this will be around the 8th of February. Between this time and the 5th of March, your beauty may not need any enhancements, because your natural attractiveness will shine forth. You can expect many admirers to come out of the woodwork during this interval.

There are some Eastern astrologers who believe that when a planet moves in its retrogressive motion, its powers are most effective, particularly in the case of Venus. After the 15th of May, your ruling planet does just this, which should accentuate your personal grooming, fashion and other means of making an impression on the world around you. You'll succeed through whatever measures you take to enhance your beauty at this time.

BEAUTY TIME

You should take note of some of the other dates for enhancing yourself and making sure others don't overlook you. The 22nd of July is a key date when Venus and the Sun provide you with radiant beauty.

Look out for the 25th of August, when your career will be further augmented through your looks and the clothes you wear, as well as the 22nd of September, the 18th of August and, once again, the 11th of November. These are dates when your ruler, Venus, gives you distinct lifts in your desire to be recognised.

On the 6th of December, when Venus climbs your career sector, expect great joy and success. You can combine your work and pleasure at this time, and use your personal attractiveness in your search for success.

 Showing off Your Libran Traits

Each zodiac sign has its own unique power based on the elements and planets that rule it. Unfortunately, most people don't know how to tap into this power and bring out their greatest potential to achieve success in life.

This year, Libra, I would suggest that you don't hide your talents, especially because your ruling planet, Venus, commences its cycle in your zone of creativity, entertainment, sport and competitiveness.

You must show off a little and let others know what you're made of. By beginning the year like this, you will set the trend for success. The power to express who you are is important most of the time, but it can be greatly enhanced through the connection with the greater benefits of Jupiter in 2012.

When is this likely to happen, you ask. Just after the 5th of March. Not only will you have the opportunity to parade your creative power, but your sexual prowess will be at an all-time high. The combined influence of Venus and Jupiter makes you very lucky, and even those accustomed to your charms, will notice something different about you at this time.

Apart from your abilities in art, painting, music and design, your skill in communication is particularly potent, because you are an air sign. In April, May, June and July you will find your mediation skills called upon to assist others.

Once again, your ruling planet will be in reverse motion, which empowers you, and you can gain a great deal of respect not just from those close to you, but from those not that familiar with you, and even strangers.

You will radiate your best traits at this time. In August and September, you bring some of your personal charm to the workplace, and I believe it is here that your year reaches its pinnacle. Don't hold back, and give it all you've got, confident that Venus will hold you in good stead in 2012.

Best Ways to Celebrate

When you celebrate your birthday, anniversary and other important events, it's important for friends and loved ones to understand that the Libran temperament is not always excited about surprises, especially if many people are going to embarrass them.

With your spiritual and creative planet, Neptune, visiting Aquarius, which relates to all things progressive, and which is in close association with Venus in the entertainment zone of your horoscope, your celebrations this year may be rather unusual, to say the least.

You might choose to celebrate through developing your Internet skills and other technological capabilities. Video games and other forms of entertainment you share with your family may be an ongoing way to celebrate life itself. But let's not limit your celebrations to one, two or three days of the year. My recommendation is that every day should be a celebration of life, which you can do this year with Venus in the position that it is.

You will want to be a little bit zany this year, and that's shown by the position of Uranus in your area of relationships and public relations. You may be tired of doing the same old thing, so this is a year when you can choose something a little different, particularly around the time of your birthday, in September or October. Let's take a look at what's happening in the heavens at the time of your solar return (which we call your birthday) for what might make your celebrations that little bit different, shall we?

At this time, there may be a tug-of-war between openly celebrating with many people, as shown by Venus in the upper or more public part of your horoscope, and privately, as shown by the Sun and Mercury in the hidden part of your zodiac. What you could do here, Libra, is try to combine a quiet and spiritual atmosphere with a few close friends, and perhaps bring in some tarot readers, psychics or other clairvoyants to create a truly entertaining yet enlightening experience for yourself and those you love.

POWER OF JUPITER

Finally, Jupiter, the natural benefactor and jovial planet of the zodiac, transits your zone of travels and higher learning in the last three months of the year. Why not travel, especially somewhere a little exotic, to celebrate your birthday or Christmas? This should be a thoroughly enjoyable time, and one that could be an eye-opener as well.

KARMA, SPIRITUALITY AND EMOTIONAL ❦ BALANCE ❦

The planets that rule your spirituality and personal growth are Mercury, Saturn and Uranus. Mercury rules your past karma, and determines some of the lessons you must learn in this life. Fortunately, in this sector of your horoscope, particularly in the last part of the year, when Jupiter enters this zone, you can expect some of the fruits of your past actions to ripen, and that may be an unexpected bonus.

Uranus, this year, spends all of its time in your zone of marriage, relationships and public relations. You'll be particularly keen to consider this aspect of your future, and when Venus enters this zone, making contact with your future karmic planet in March, you will experience clarity—albeit a shock—when you come to some new realisations about what you want.

Another important time is the cycle of Saturn after the 5th of October. Your thinking will be very much focused on money, and on the karmic consequences of how you use your hard-earned cash. Sharing your resources will also be more important to you at this time.

Uranus, the signifier of your future karma, moves direct in motion on the 13th of December. Many of your personal questions about philosophy, religion and spiritual self-actualisation will become clearer at that time.

DOING GOOD FOR OTHERS

Doing good for others is part of accumulating karmic Brownie points, if I could put it that way. During this cycle, especially in April, May and June, your spiritual sense will be strong, and you can bring this to your workplace to help others who, in turn, will help you. As the old saying goes, 'What goes around, comes around', and this is true for you, Libra, in the year of 2012.

2012
MONTHLY & DAILY PREDICTIONS

A SOLDIER WILL FIGHT LONG AND
HARD FOR A BIT OF COLOURED
RIBBON.

Napoleon

❀ JANUARY ❀

 Monthly Highlight

Although you feel somewhat weighed down by your day-to-day responsibilities, Venus still affords you the opportunity to feel loving, amorous and in the mood for love. January should indeed be a time when romantic opportunities arise, especially for singles, bringing you great satisfaction.

Domestic issues change, and a new phase for family life commences.

---

1 You may find a safe haven in a love union today, strengthening you or diverting you from any unpleasant issues in your relationships.

---

2 Although it may seem surprising, your work is likely to serve as a source of satisfaction for you during this period. Clients are enamoured by you, too.

---

3 This is a fortunate and prosperous time, as job-related goals and financial activities turn out to be productive or promising. Tax is an issue, however.

---

4   If you are single, you may have an opportunity to mix business with pleasure, or to meet a suitable mate through your employment. Your sexuality is powerful under these transits.

5   You might notice that your focus has shifted to the prospect of love or a primary romantic relationship at the moment. But your philosophies must meld.

6   An enthusiastic or whole-hearted approach to your studies is indicated, and is one way that you can express yourself to the world just now.

7   You will give the impression today that you are seeking more fulfilment, commitment, stability and teamwork in life. Don't be afraid to express your deepest yearnings.

8   You will go that extra mile today, ensuring you can be relied upon to deliver any promises, pledges or obligations in the area of work. An employer is pleased with your efforts.

9   If you are out of work at moment, your earnest search for a meaningful professional path may be successful today.

10 This period will more than likely bring forward an increased need for security in both job-related and financial affairs. Extra cash is likely.

11 Inattentiveness, disinterest or a sense that something is lacking in your social life or current love affair is likely just now. Listen with your *heart* as well as your ears.

12 Difficult rifts and tension can occur within a close relationship today, as you become distracted by other interests and involvements.

13 You are inclined to waver or be indecisive in your obligations and reliability—as far as love and romance is concerned—at present, so reassure your partner.

14 Beware of a tendency to over-react, or of trying to force your intentions on others, regardless of the appropriateness of your actions.

15 It is necessary to make a concerted effort to give more time to your relationships, but without sacrificing your own needs in the process.

16 Positive influences arise just now, giving you the chance to work through your troubles in a relationship or personal matter.

17 Healing and the resolution of particular issues can begin by training your heart to give and receive more. Finances feature strongly at the moment, so remember the theme on this point.

18 A current business partner can bring you a newfound awareness and understanding of your true values and material desires. Balance this with a loving approach.

19 You will draw to yourself the aid and guidance needed to remove blocks within your mental, emotional or spiritual lives today. But once the answer arrives, the question is, will you be prepared to act on it?

20 Take care not to neglect your business, and to use good judgement when signing contracts or agreements. You needn't say yes at the drop of a hat. Move slowly on professional matters.

21 Your intuitive abilities will expand, and it's a good time to start practices such as meditation, prayer, or connecting more closely with your spiritual beliefs. A family matter is annoying.

21 You will become agreeable and pleasant to family members, much to their surprise. Improve your family relationships today.

22 This is a day in which you will concentrate on expressing your talents more freely. Competitive activities are also appealing, so sports or games of chance might also be on your agenda.

23 You won't feel like arguing or competing with anyone today, but may still do well in sports or other outdoor activities.

24 You will be interested improving your personal image at the moment, including your presentation, clothing and diet. Work on an exercise regime that fits your current lifestyle.

25 You will concentrate your efforts on acquiring beautiful things and be attracted to luxuries today, but debts could mount if you are not prudent in your spending. Tighten your belt a little.

26 Workplace activities can be overwhelming as you try to arrange a new schedule. Someone may disagree with you and cause you some angst.

27 If you are currently a bit detached from your spouse or partner, you will need to make them feel more relaxed before being able to express your emotions more freely.

28 Due to your charming attitude, many people will be attracted to you today, and this could overinflate your ego. Maintain humility, even if you become the god or goddess of your peers for the time being.

29 You are looking for authority and importance in your life, but if you redirect some of your energies, you will achieve and fulfil your destiny. Transformative exercises like yoga will help you manage these energies.

30 You might be explosive about abrupt changes in your financial matters, especially if you are in some sort of partnership. Speak clearly and without emotion today.

31 Your mood can quickly change from one of pleasure-seeking to serious business acumen today. It may seem like day turning into night, but this is good, because you realise it is time to get 'back to the grindstone'.

❄ FEBRUARY ❄

 Monthly Highlight

Your energy may be low this month, even though your creative urges are still strong. This is a month to take stock of yourself before rushing headlong into new enterprises.

Mars and Venus cause you to be impulsive, sexually and romantically. There may be secrets that emerge, and the possibility of your jealousy being aroused is quite likely.

1 Life won't be dull today, especially in your romance and sexual experiences. It's important to spend quality time with the one you love, and not let other partnerships overlap with your private life.

2 The vibrations of those around you are of mixed calibre today, as you try to sort the genuine from the fake. Use your intellect and intuitive powers to discriminate. You can dream and plan your travels today as well.

3 Consider moving if you're not comfortable where you're currently living. You may not be able to do it overnight, but taking the time to consider the options is important just now.

4 Do you doubt yourself, especially what you're doing in your work? Let go of past projects that may not have gone to plan. Use your energy and willpower to forge a new path now.

5 It's time to embrace change professionally— you mustn't be nervous about it. You can use dramatic flair, and elements of power and control—rather than a pleasing personality—to get what you want.

6 Don't let others cry all over you. Your compassion may be abused at present, because those with powerful ambitions may be using every ploy possible to get you to help them further their career.

7 You have to be a little bit rebellious if you want to make headway in your personal life, and in particularly your social sphere. You're getting tired of the same old, same old at the moment.

8 You need to be patient with a friend just now, to help them be realistic in their aims. Apart from considering *their* needs, you should look at what your own requirements are. Life is, of course, about give and take.

9 Be patient in achieving your dreams and ambitions. It's time to take stock of yourself. Today may not be a day for action, but rather, for planning.

10 Although you desire to be loved by one and all, it's not forthcoming just now, and this could cause you to get angry. Your fiery emotions may come out at the most inappropriate moment today.

11 Your concern for others may not be recognised at present. It could make you feel upset that you're not being appreciated, so why not think of creative ways to get the recognition you desire?

12 Look after your spiritual side as well as the material things in life at the moment. Start to live your life independently and do things your own way, rather than as others would have you do them.

13 You're curious about money just now, but may be cautious in trying something a little different. Dare to attempt something out of the ordinary.

14 You can use your agreeable personality to tap into moneymaking powers that can help you get ahead at the moment. The focus today is quality, not quantity.

15 You are restless at the moment, and attracted to many different things. However, your versatility may be your undoing. Focus on just one thing.

16 You mustn't let work dominate you and your life. Get a quiet hobby with no demands—this will bring peace and quiet to the whirlwind of your professional life.

17 Be active and passionate (but not impulsive) when it comes to dealing with matters on the home front today. Someone at home is being intolerant, and this could cause you to compromise your integrity.

18 The Sun is shining brightly on you at the moment, bringing power and success. Real estate, home affairs and other investments should be looked at today.

19 You're doing everyone else's work and it's time to put your foot down. Others have time on their hands, too; get them to do their fair share.

20 You may be wearing out a lot of people with your high ideals and creative energy today. Try going one step at a time, especially if you want them to understand you.

21 Everything is changing for you just now, and you're interested in creating some new relationships. Romance is in the air, so go for it, Libra!

22 Your energy at work could be overwhelming, and you may be a little too forceful today. Use your quick-wittedness and humour to endear yourself to the less energetic souls around you.

23 One hundred and ten per cent is your starting point with any projects right now, and that's how you must approach your relationships as well. Full commitment—and nothing less—is what is needed.

24 High creativity and imagination should be applied to your relationships at the moment. Your partner may be lazy in doing their share of the emotional work. Coax them up to a level of equality.

25 You know that no amount of material acquisition will satisfy your need for inner security. That goes for relationships as well. Having someone in your life doesn't necessarily mean you've found that emotional fulfilment.

26 Assertion is not the same as aggression, and if you can learn the difference, your relationships will be better off. Use your powers of persuasion to get what you want today.

27 Your strong stamina and libido could be a problem for your partner as you demand more than they can give. This requires finding an additional outlet for your primal urges.

28 Bottling up resentment and guilt is holding you back. The battle for time between home and family needs to be balanced so that everyone gets their fair share of you.

29 You must evaluate a new situation before making a decision. Once you've done that, get on with it and let go of the past. Never carry remorse around with you. This is the start of a new cycle.

❋ MARCH ❋

Monthly Highlight

Issues surrounding long-term commitments, marriage and significant business partnerships will take pride of place on your agenda this month. You'll be working through differences of opinion, but also planning for a clearer future based on your personal needs.

Work could become overwhelming as you take on too much. Debts and other financial concerns will need to be dealt with effectively and without emotion.

You want to spend big and reward yourself for some good work, and feel it's time to appreciate yourself with confidence.

---

1. At present, neither luxurious surroundings nor anything money can buy is satisfying you. You realise there's more to life, and 'Material Girl' is no longer your theme song. Spirituality seems to be a new interest.

---

2 You're positively electric today, and will attract unusual people who can help you better understand life. Your karma is strong and good people will come to you just now.

3 Your lightning-speed thoughts, combined with your people skills, are excellent in propelling you forward in your business life. There are some successful opportunities around or, at least, you can see them on the horizon.

4 You can work from home for a while if you wish, and with your energy and love of family life strong at the moment, this could be the ideal solution to balancing home and business interests.

5 You need to use your psychic ability to separate friends from secret enemies. You have an intuition that all is not right in your peer group just now. Trust your hunches.

6 You mustn't plan yourself into a standstill, especially if others are pushing you to move forward. A social event may delay others upon whom you are relying.

7 Keep a solid wall between your personal and business relationships. Otherwise, trouble will brew. You must not aim your energies in too many directions at once.

8   There are skeletons in the closet for all of us, but if you're living in the past, you're missing the present. You could feel down today, when there's no need to. Look forwards, not backwards.

9   Once again, you're feeling restless and trying to reach for something that may be an illusion. Express gratitude for what you have, rather than desire what you don't.

10 You're in the mood for pleasure and luxury, but you mustn't take any additional cash for granted, because you could squander it. Hold on to it for the moment, and spend wisely.

11 You want to be comfortable in both your work and your home, so you'll need extra money, and possibly an additional job, to cover this. Don't run yourself into the ground, though—you need to balance your desires against the sacrifice required.

12 Money continues to be a theme over the next few days. Your highly tuned sense of what's available should be trusted, because you have the opportunity to create a separate source of income, or at least plan for it.

13 Even though you love to look good and make an impression on others, today you may not be up to it. To develop your power and leadership qualities, you may need to take some time out.

14 Contracts are important just now, so don't follow your heart without giving your head a fair degree of latitude to assist your decisions. Read between the lines.

15 Your thinking processes are about making plans, but is anyone around you listening? You may be off with the fairies while others have different ideas. Consultation is necessary.

16 The opposite sex is pretty impressed with you today, but you've got responsibilities on the home front, so what are you going to do? You may need to postpone an engagement.

17 If you've got a hunch, act on it. Especially if it involves someone in your family. You'll notice that something is wrong with someone you love. Try drawing them out of their shell.

18 You have love for someone but may not be able to express it. Why not ask a go-between to bridge the gap between you and this person?

19 If you're looking for an improvement in your relationship, a little less vinegar and a little more honey will give your partner a chance to say what's on their mind.

20 The wheel of fortune's spinning your way, and if you're not happy at work, it's time to take advantage of what else is being offered or directed. Take a gamble.

21 You need a chill pill today if you've been finding it difficult and stressful at work. Someone is forcing a decision, and you may not be able to handle the pressure.

22 Are you the treasurer of your group? Are you handling money on behalf of others? You need to be above reproach, otherwise the finger of blame may be pointed at you.

23 You could be stuck in a time warp and afraid of change, especially with your partner. If the one you love is trying to move forward and you've got your heels dug into the ground, there is no way for the two of you to progress. Flexibility is the key word.

24 Your body may be sending you the signal to rest, but instead you're burning the candle at both ends. Friends could cause you to spread yourself too thinly. Containment lines are necessary.

25 While others are basking in the warmth of your personality, are you really getting the responses you need from them? A transformation can take place when you realise that relationships are two-way streets.

26 Think before giving away something of importance, even if it's out of a deep compassion for your fellow humans. Your intentions are noble, but this may not be a wise move.

27 If you're seeking fame, power and money, and ignoring the simple things in life, the equation is imbalanced. Moderation in all areas is the secret of true success.

28 Meditation will give you a sense of peace and could dilute your tendency to steamroll everyone around you. Try quiet assertion; this will be much better.

29 You need to ease up on yourself, because you've probably been demanding more than you can give. It's okay to slow the pace occasionally, irrespective of what others are expecting.

30 Your life could feel like it's in a constant state of change at the moment. But just be mindful that others are not as quick off the mark as you. Timing is everything in your work, especially today.

31 You need to put a little money aside for a rainy day, especially if you're feeling apprehensive about the security of your work.

❋ APRIL ❋

Monthly Highlight

There is a strong sexual tone to this month, and your physical drives are strong. The new Moon appearing in your zone of deep emotional and personal transformation means there are significant lessons that you and your spouse, partner or lover may experience this month.

1 It's time to enjoy the company of friends, but also to work a little on your creative abilities. Find that quiet place within yourself, and stop worrying about others.

2 Are you being offered a way to get rich quickly? Stay well away from it, and rely on your intuition to look after your money. The work you do will help you accumulate money slowly but surely.

3 Get your moods under control, even if someone you love needs a kick in the pants. Exercising restraint will help them more than if you get angry at them.

4   It's time to consider getting more involved with artistic, musical or cultural activities, especially in your home. You have a sense of beauty, colour and harmony just now, so use it to design something.

5   If you've got the urge to travel, you may be missing an opportunity by postponing it. Start to plan, even if it's not going to be an immediate thing. This will be enjoyable.

6   You're not the fastest person to make a decision, and you could well be oscillating today. Missed opportunities may occur due to your slow responses.

7   Don't alienate your friends and colleagues because of your sharp tongue. A little sugar-coating will go a long way towards maintaining their respect.

8   It's a brave soul who boldly goes where no one else has gone before. Today, we're talking about money again. By all means, take a punt. But make sure you have all your facts first.

9   You have the power of persuasion, and your discussions and conversations will be met with great respect just now. However, stay clear of idle gossip.

10 Other people are placing great faith in you, and your ability to tell it as it is will help them. You must, however, remember that everyone is at different levels and stages of progress.

11 You need to monitor and prioritise time just now, because you have too much stuff on your plate. You'll be scattering your energies everywhere, at the risk of getting nowhere at all.

12 Your creative potential and charisma can be further enhanced by selecting the finest clothing. If you're a born leader, then look like a leader.

13 Today is one of patience, and this is not always an easy virtue to develop. Someone's deliberately pressing your buttons, so you'll certainly be tested.

14 You need your well-balanced nature and sound judgement to deal with a child or younger person in your vicinity. Having said that, don't bite off more than you can chew. You may promise them more than you can deliver.

15 Have your own opinions but don't forget, especially in a new relationship, that they may scare someone. Go slowly before revealing all.

16 Once again, you need to slow down and try to stay in one place a little bit longer. You're saying yes to everyone, taking on more responsibilities than you should, and finding out very quickly that fatigue is setting in.

17 Striving for worldly success and happiness in personal relationships may be undermined by your need to work competitively just now. Something has to give. What will it be?

18 Yours is the number people call at work, but some of the problems brewing there are not of your making, so why should you sort them out? Political troubles are at hand.

19 Your success can only be brought about by a balance of strong ambition, a sense of purpose, and consideration for your partner. Talk about what you both want, and find the common ground.

20 If you're considering changing your workplace or residence, you need to work from an intellectual rather than instinctive standpoint. Also, stop listening to others and trying to keep up with the Joneses. That's the wrong motivation.

21 You're excited and inspired by someone just now, but suppressing your feelings could result in physical problems. Let it all out, Libra!

22 You could put your hand to writing just now. This is a way to delve into your past and resolve some of the emotional complexities within you. Putting your feelings on paper will also help if you're feeling a little down.

23 The power of your insight can impress others, especially when it comes to joint finances and business deals. Play down your tendency to exaggerate, because there is a limit to what others will believe today.

24 Your very generous nature will tax your physical system to its limits. Giving to others is fine, but you run the risk of burning out if you don't also give to yourself.

25 Your wheeling and dealing skills are great just now, and some lucky breaks will come your way. But learn to know how to recognise them.

26 Barriers at work are not something you handle very well. Professional relationships should give you the freedom you need to be who you are and to work in the way you want. Express these feelings today.

27 To your own self be true, and always maintain that sense of self. You don't have to reflect a mirror image to those around you, and you should stay clear of any negativity.

28 Let the past be just that—the past. In some workplace negotiations, you may need to deal with someone who has left an unpleasant taste in your mouth. Clean your slate and begin afresh for the best results.

29 You shoot from the lip, and others can find this confronting just now. Being brutally honest, however, means that people will have no doubts about where you stand on a particular issue.

30 Centre stage is where you should be at present, but it can be a lonely place. The support you need from friends may not be all that you had expected.

Monthly Highlight

You have the urge to travel, but may be distracted by those who oppose your independence—this time, family members and even close friends. They may feel as if they are missing out on something you are planning. Alleviate their fears and enjoy yourself.

1   You need to redirect some of the pent-up energies you're feeling into better outlets today. You're angry at someone, but can't say anything. Maybe cleaning the house will help?

2   You are displaying some of your rather eccentric tastes today, which could make people around you a little nervous because they don't know where you're coming from. Assure them there's nothing to be worried about.

3   Never fear change, because, in your case, this is a big year and you'll want to make some radical moves just now. Balance is the key word.

4 Your divided loyalties between profession and family can cause you some angst. Try to involve those you love with what you do so they can better understand what it entails.

5 You seem to know when someone needs help just now, and you'll even be willing to lend them some money. Don't give more than you've got, however, as you'll leave nothing for yourself.

6 Today, you need some help, but are too proud to ask someone for it. You'll feel as if you're imposing. Actually, people like to be asked for help, so try it.

7 You could jump to a conclusion about your partner and then have to quickly backpedal when you realise you've made an incorrect assumption. Scrutinise your motivations rather than simply snapping into action.

8 Anything to do with money or your career just now requires you to plan more carefully. Knee-jerk reactions are certainly not needed.

9 Have you lost where you're heading lately? Get back in tune with your inner self, and regain your sense of self-identity, otherwise confusion will continue to reign supreme.

10 Higher education or perhaps a home-study course will be a source of great fortune to you in the future. Your love of humanity is also be part of the mix. Consider how you can expand your mental horizons.

11 Your mood swings can cause you to feel depressed and elated in the one day at the moment. You need to look at what's causing these extreme shifts. Perhaps it's your diet?

12 Be careful today, because people may try to use you to bolster their own security. They could put you down as a way of lifting themselves up. Don't react to such things.

13 You're probably using your professional workload as an escape from personal problems, which is no way to resolve these issues. Face up to the problem and solve it, because you know how to.

14 Your rather direct way of speaking to someone today could alienate them, and you may not know why. Try being more conscientious—stand in the other person's shoes.

15 Telling tall tales doesn't always ring true in the minds of others, and you run the risk of ruining your reputation with them. If you're honest today, the results will be far more promising.

16 Surround yourself with those who cherish you. You've been selling yourself short lately, so distance yourself from those who are not going to give you the love and honour you deserve.

17 You may need a deep and meaningful with your lover to tell them exactly how you're feeling. You've been saying yes, when you really mean no. If your being taken for granted, it's time for that to stop.

18 Shared money is important just now, so be clear about what you expect from those with whom you've pooled resources. Under no circumstances marry for money, either.

19 You'll need to be a bit of a control freak just now, because someone has been slack in the way they manage finances. You need to bring forth some commercial aggression to make things right.

20 Money maketh the man, or so the saying goes. Issues surrounding control—and the way you use money to bring people into line—could become an issue, and may blow up in your face around this time.

21 Looking at your past becomes more interesting to you now as you try to find out about your genealogy, family history and the people who made you who you are.

22 You could feel a little isolated today, as your philosophical views help you realise the true meaning of life. Don't get too caught up with these things, and keep life practical as well.

23 Relationships can be stormy, and for those of you who work with their partners, this could be a volatile day. Watch your stress levels, and if they get too high, enjoy some sex or perhaps even meditation.

24 There's a highly creative energy around you, and you are showing a distinct skill in your work. Others may recognise this but won't necessarily say anything. Ask for feedback.

25 You need harmony in your workplace if you're going to feel satisfied with what you're doing. Demand it, especially if there are distractive elements causing you problems.

26 Enjoy some music and art with friends. Even if you're not expressive in this way, being in the company of those who are will lift your spirits.

27 Making money is not what you worship as your god, but it sure can help to ease the problems in life. Look at ways to enhance your earning capacity today.

28 You need to be more tactful and diplomatic in dealing with others, and not be too proud to ask for help. Pick your mark carefully, because someone you approach may initially feel irritable or frustrated with you.

29 Your sense of identity is not that strong today, so you should determine what's undermining it. Try to have a quiet talk with someone you trust. That will help.

30 Are you clinging to something you should have let go of a long time ago—for example, a relationship? Your tendency to be nurturing just now may be holding you back.

31 Aim high and, even if things don't work out quite as planned, your optimism will act as a buffer and help you get through a difficult day.

❋ JUNE ❋

 Monthly Highlight

Higher educational pursuits, expanding your horizons, and generally investigating new cultures and opportunities in life will excite you this month. Your mind is intensely stimulated, and you will need others to support you in this. Otherwise, have no fear of treading your life path alone for awhile.

---

1 You may have already been given an answer to your question, so don't keep asking it—you could blow it. Be content with what's offered.

---

2 Your inner being needs as much nurturing as your outer requirements dictate. You could be focusing too much on how you look and what you have, rather than simply on who you are.

---

3 You need to be a little mysterious and enigmatic if you're trying to conduct business or get someone onside just now. A little mystery will go a long way.

---

4 Your work and marriage issues may need delicate handling, because your desirous nature is blocking out everyone else's needs. This could be a selfish day, so try to tone it down.

5 Don't hide the sensitive side of your nature behind a screen of competitiveness and invincibility. If you show your vulnerability to others, your softness will help win over their hearts.

6 Power is an awesome weapon, but you mustn't use it to disadvantage others. It should also not be used to overcome your emotional difficulties. Healthy emotions should always be your focus.

7 If you want your own space for a while, that may be difficult to arrange—others are cramming you and demanding a lot of your time. You may need to leave the house to create a little bit of personal room today.

8 Being a thinker and a planner can be a creative activity for you right now. You have some ideas, but it's probably best not to share them just yet.

9 Try to get more of a social life happening for yourself, especially if you've been overworking. Learning how to win friends and influence people is important, because ultimately this will help your work as well.

10 Your creative energy is in abundance, and this gives you great leadership potential, especially in a work-related field. Having said that, try not to be unrealistic about what's possible.

11 You have an enemy around at the moment, and your softness might give them an opening to damage you. You need to disarm them before finding out their motives.

12 You have a strong desire for something very different at the moment, due to the Moon and Uranus. There's an electric vibration around you that will cause you to be impulsive. Think twice before acting.

13 You could attract some rather unusual people into your life due to a high-pressure situation in which you're currently involved. You could be running away from the situation, rather than facing up to it fairly and squarely.

14 You need to do one thing at a time, and try to do it well, Libra. By cutting corners, you'll end up spending much more time on the tasks than is necessary.

15 Powerful women could be a part of your life today, but don't fear them. Someone may help you with advice or an introduction that will speed up the process of success.

16 You may be driven to take an unusual sidetrack in your life at the moment, but you should always maintain a clear direction and purpose. This could have been triggered by something you heard.

17 You need to invest more time in the art of communication or in extending your knowledge base in your field of endeavour. A study course or seminar may be in order.

18 Make it clear whether you're protecting your family and friends or just being domineering. They may not be able to decipher your actions otherwise.

19 You mustn't force others to do things against their will. There may be a philosophical or moral principle at stake today.

20 You know that no one is an island unto themselves, so you mustn't isolate yourself. You'll bring out the best in others if you're involved with them and their lives, and if you actively participate in what's going on.

21 Don't demand your partner be something they're not. You need to deepen your understanding of the word acceptance just now.

22 Improve your temperament, and you'll see the results in your home life as well. The example you set to your partner and your children will be exhibited in their behaviour in due course.

23 Try to savour the moment you're in at present, because you're trying to experience too much too quickly. This will require patience, but will be well worth the wait.

24 Flexibility is important today, for this could be a time when you remain stubborn only to be left out in the cold. Adjust yourself to others.

25 Humanitarian activities might attract you today. Someone in need could be the trigger for this.

26 You're feeling like a bit of a loner at this stage, so don't involve yourself in too much at present. You won't require others' input either, so kindly decline their invitations.

27 Keep a lid on your explosive nature, because you're feeling frustrated by life generally. Control yourself and learn restraint.

28 You're feeling conservative at the moment, and even if you want to do something bold, Saturn will not allow it. In the end, your traditional attitude will provide you a better angle.

29 Although you have financial power, you must not abuse it lest it blow up on you. Share your power with others to make them feel comfortable in their association with you.

30 You need to lighten up in your dealings with others, especially children. You may be over-reacting in your meting out of punishment. Don't be a tyrant.

❊ JULY ❊

 Monthly Highlight

This should be one of the most social months of the year, with the new Moon bringing opportunities to expand your circle of friends and acquaintances. Mercury brings with it an opportunity to explore new avenues of communication and mix with some fascinating new people.

Try not to think of negative issues this month, because that will only serve to bring you down. Keep everything light and breezy.

1 You need to overcome your fear of change to believe that any movement forward is positive. Even if you perceive obstacles, your success will be achieved only through change.

2 What you imagine about someone else is actually pretty far from the truth. Look at your friend today with non-judgemental eyes.

3 You've got the determination and concentration to achieve many things just now, but something's holding you back. Procrastination is a great destroyer of success because it makes you miss out on valuable opportunities.

4 You have a critical mind today, and the way you deliver your opinions could cause a backlash from your loved ones. Use your speech constructively. Diplomacy and tact are necessary.

5 There's a daring quality about you today. You should direct your competitive streak into such things as sport or games of chance.

6 Your highly intuitive and imaginative way of presenting ideas will convince people of the benefits of being with you. This is a positive day.

7 People trust you, and right now you have the ability to help them and, in the process, help yourself. Collaborative professional work is favoured.

8 You may decide to choose a partner for future professional activities during this period. Take the time to scrutinise potential business associates carefully.

9 People are gravitating towards you at the moment, but what's the reason for that? You're probably feeling flattered, when, in fact, they're trying to use you.

10 Sometimes, your mood swings will be a little hard for others to keep up with, and that's the case today. You need a direct approach when dealing with others, and should call a spade, a spade.

11 You may be experiencing some hard times between you and your partner, but you should see this as an opportunity for growth rather than as an inhibition. There may be a bit of a cool attitude towards each other, but this will pass.

12 You have an explosive edge today, and you need to be careful how you direct that energy. You're a powder keg of ideas, and that can make for an incredibly exciting life. But you need someone with which to share it.

13 Research is important to you just now, and that could be in any number of areas: relationships, work, finances and yourself. Delve deeply.

14 It's not a good thing to be unhappily in love. This is not at all practical, and is a waste of time and life. If you're unhappy in a relationship, get out of it.

15 Your mind is unusual now, and you have the uncanny ability to feel the depths of others. Your intuition is growing. Spiritual matters take precedence.

16 If you're single, you may have to be patient and wait for the right person to come along. If you're being cynical about love and marriage, that's not going to help your chances. Remain open, and attract someone great into your life.

17 It's okay to use a blunt approach with someone, but with your explosive ideas, you run the risk of others thinking that you're striking too heavily. Be gentle.

18 Your vitality is attracting assistance just now, and radiant help should hold you in good stead. Use these creative energies to win some Brownie points with your boss.

19 What about keeping company with not only uplifting people, but those who are better than yourself? Put aside your ego, and let their expertise help you get to the next level. You can learn a lot from them.

20 It may take a while, but you'll get to your destination eventually, and remember, you need to surround yourself with the right people. You could feel short-changed by a friend just now.

21 It's great to be relied upon, but not necessarily leaned upon. Someone is expecting you to do something at their pace, and you need to correct them on the terms. Your schedule should be based on your work, not theirs.

22 Let go of your bottled-up tensions and any resentments, otherwise they will affect your health. Take a day or two off.

23 You may be gambling, and even if it's only for fun, you may find yourself losing a little money. Hold on to your wallet, because you could misplace things today.

24 You're worried about money or, rather, the accumulation of it, and that energy can delay your financial success. You need to love what you're doing, and forget about what you're earning.

25 Putting some trust into your marriage or relationship is essential just now. If you analyse the reason for its absence, it may stem from a bad experience in your past. Once again, let go, and live in the clear, present moment.

26 You're appearing a little hard-hearted to others, but you have your reasons for it. High-risk activities are not for you today.

27 You could challenge authority today, but that might bring a swift retaliation. Unless you're sure you can win the war, be careful which battles you pick.

28 There's imagination that is creative, and that which is just daydreaming. Know the difference. Your fantasies should have a practical plan and immense willpower behind them.

29 Express your concepts and any unusual ideas in a way that is acceptable to others. Considering a profession in a creative field might also be appealing just now.

30 You must stop contemplating ideas and get moving. There's no point counting the number of leaves on a mango tree if you're hungry for the fruit. Pick the mango and eat it, I say.

31 Health, hygiene and hospitality are the three H-words today. Work at home to bring these three issues into focus. It will make for a happier family unit.

✳ AUGUST ✳

Monthly Highlight

You may experience poor a self-image this month, notwithstanding the fact that others find you fascinating, attractive and someone they want to be around. Privately, you will need to work on your self-esteem, and find appropriate outlets for your increasing tensions and frustration.

1 You have strong feelings, but may also be frustrated by Mars and Saturn. Use these energies constructively rather than feeling thwarted. You'll produce something wonderful that way.

2 Even though others need your help, you shouldn't offer it unsolicited. There are ways to help them through more subtle means at the moment.

3 It's time to stop and smell the roses, and if you do, it's not time wasted. You need to develop the quality of trust just now, especially with the full Moon.

4 You mustn't make the mistake of becoming a slave to your work practices. You could become the sacrificial lamb, playing the role of martyr. Stop being the victim.

5 Someone may let you down and, if meeting a deadline is dependent on them, this could cause you some problems. Have a Plan B in place before you commence.

6 You carry the past with you and must learn to let go, otherwise you run the risk of not seeing things for what they really are. I'm talking about a relationship here. It's time to move forward.

7 Relationships could get you down during this time, with Mars and Saturn hammering the Moon. You may not know whether you're Arthur or Martha, coming or going, wanting or not wanting. Stop, think, and then proceed.

8 The person you carry on your arm must reflect your good taste and be seen as classy company. You could feel uncomfortable about someone whose standards are not as high as yours.

9 You don't want instability just now, so you are likely to push something to the limits to test its breakability. A friendship could be fragile and might crack under the pressure.

2012 MONTHLY & DAILY PREDICTIONS | 159

10 You have luck on your side, but you mustn't rely wholly and solely on this one factor. Hard work plus good fortune will carry you across the finishing line.

11 Lately, you've been a social dynamo, but by the same token, you may be feeling uncomfortable about the calibre of the people with whom you're associating. It may be time for a change.

12 You're able to grasp ideas without any mental effort just now. It's a great time to enjoy new educational pursuits. This is a fun period for learning and personal growth.

13 You need a partner in life who can understand what you want to achieve in your work. Venus now gives you a great deal of popularity, but make sure your partner doesn't become jealous.

14 Your job may make you feel more like a welfare worker as you take on the responsibilities of others who are less capable. Delegate some of their tasks to get through your own.

15 Success in your endeavours is likely after an initial period of trial and intense work. However, beware of negativity—this could lead to pessimism, and darken your business affairs.

16 It's a great time of social satisfaction, with the Sun and Mercury affecting your social sphere. Your personality's strong, but you may meet someone just as strong.

17 Your strong personality and excellent attractiveness are your greatest assets today, and your social circle should expand accordingly. Enjoy parties, functions and simply hanging out with good people.

18 Life could be a bit of a rollercoaster ride at the moment, and your moods are well in keeping with it. Education, training and spiritual awareness are your key words today.

19 Hot gossip is tantalising, but also damaging to others and, who knows, even to yourself. Don't get involved in malicious talk behind other people's backs.

20 If your self-image has been a little lacking, you can develop it just now, and confidently step forward for what you want. A cautious approach is necessary, however. Underplay your brilliance.

21 Even if you take pride in your independence today, you may find someone stifling you. Try to see how this might be of benefit to you, rather than simply resisting it.

22 Your good intentions and your ability with words will give you success in sales and marketing today. Even if this is not your job, you may need to tap into these resources for something you desire.

23 You may not quite be making the right connections with others to further your business needs. Successful networking is important at this moment.

24 If you've got unresolved issues of love and closeness that stem from parental involvement, they may resurface in your relationship over the next few days. Investigate them without any bias.

25 You're bold and headstrong and insensitively so. You can learn a lot from being humble for a while. Slow and steady wins the race.

26 If you use a softer speaking manner, this will help you avoid potential trouble with your business or marriage partner. Dispute and litigation are in the air, therefore more honey and less vinegar is needed.

27 It's time for you to move forward if you're planning any changes on the home front. Purchasing a new house may be hindered by of offloading your current property. On another level, it could simply be time for a facelift of your current residence. A change is as good as a holiday.

28 You will achieve your ambitions eventually, but may feel a delay as a result of a conflict of interest with your children or family. You need to put your heads together and find a solution to eliminate this problem.

29 Your exceptional talent should be manipulated wisely to bring out the best outcomes for all involved. Watch out for rivalry in your workplace, however.

30 You can easily predict financial trends at the moment, but should make this an advantage to yourself, not just to others. If someone else has a windfall, make sure you get a cut of the spoils.

31 There could be a problem attending a party where a rival will also be present. You can either not go, or go—it's your choice. If you do go, remember to downplay the importance of that person.

SEPTEMBER

Monthly Highlight

With your antagonists out of the way, this month should bring you opportunities to fulfil yourself through both work and social engagements. An opportunity to elevate yourself, acquire a new job or even a promotion is on the cards.

1 Leave failure out of your vocabulary today, and instead use the word success. You may be sabotaging yourself, attracting negative situations simply by thinking of them. Change your mental strategy.

2 You mustn't give up on improving some aspect of your personal life just now. Even if your partner is reluctant to change, be persistent, and it will happen.

3 You can instil confidence in those who look up to you today. Although your success is assured after a long fight, your enemies may still create opposition and hardship. Be mindful of that.

4 Don't let the passion of the moment blind you to other valuable opportunities. You've taken your eye off the ball. Others trust you and feel your suggestions are genuinely designed for them today.

5 You won't suffer fools gladly at the moment, and having been bitten once, you'll be doubly shy. It's a good time to associate with people of rank, nobility and power to achieve your success.

6 It may seem as though getting through your workload is like climbing a mountain, but there will be an unexpected opportunity that comes your way soon. Keep your ears open and your eyes focused. Your friends are indeed fortunate, too.

7 Enhance your appearance by wearing fine clothes. It's amazing how you can lift your class a couple of notches just by the way you use colour and fashion.

8 Others will know exactly how you feel, even if what you have to say is uncomfortable. Although you want to be liked by everyone, don't set out for the sake of approval today.

9   You'll be well-respected by many people today, and this is due to your high standards and sense of fair play. You may be interested in learning how you can develop your executive ability around this time.

10   You could extend your work, but it might affect your physical wellbeing. You've been too self-critical, and this is the fuel that is pushing you. You must again give some time to your inner life.

11   There's a whirlwind in your life at present, and you mustn't move simply for the sake of moving. Spend a little more time in one place so your thoughts can catch up with you.

12   Your social surroundings need to be in harmony with your spirit. Don't put yourself into a situation that's going to be uncomfortable and adversely affect your nerves.

13   Someone may prompt you to consider a serious career change. You might want to think about areas of healing and helping others, because these could be well suited to your nature. Don't forget to nurture yourself, too, Libra.

14   Your ability with money is not so good right now, and you need to develop the skills of being resourceful and prudent. You're probably a little depressed by the fact that you have more bills than you had anticipated.

15   You've been working and playing a little too hard, and could be a bit bored as a result But sometimes boredom affords us the opportunity to see ourselves as we truly are.

16   You'll start to be more action-oriented today, but may not want to be the centre of attention. Working behind the scenes and helping someone else seems to be the order of the day.

17   You may go out of your way to impress others, but remember, all that glitters is not gold. You may not receive the accolades you had hoped for. Try to be more subtle in conveying what you think are your better points.

18   Matters of cleanliness and having a sterile environment will be important to you just now. You're bothered by the untidiness and bad habits of others. Focus on your own habits as well.

19 If you're home or job hunting, today is a day when you could find success in the form of an offer or referral. Settle for no less than what you believe is fair.

20 Earning extra money could be an upward climb just now—you're not finding it that easy to come up with the additional cash. Cutting back on expenses is the only way for you to progress.

21 Your thinking may be influenced by someone, and this could impact adversely on your family circle, which doesn't agree with you. You may need to keep your thoughts to yourself for a little while.

22 Count to ten, and breathe deeply. Something may be bogging you down and you're not getting the results you want. You may have to grin and bear the situation, because there's little you can do to alter the course that has been set.

23 Break down all the barriers between yourself and those you love. This may take time, but you'll have to make the first step.

24 There could be a few people competing for your attention at the moment, so giving them adequate love and care may not be easy. You need to prioritise one over the other for a short time.

25 Love, passion and idealism are strong focal points today, with the Moon in your zone of love affairs. You are very creative, and will enjoy the opportunity for a new relationship.

26 Commercial opportunities are staring you in the face, but you may need to take a calculated risk. A friend or younger person may be the messenger who brings you some good news.

27 Conditions are ideal for you to improve your working life by purchasing or wearing more appropriate clothing. You may also need to upgrade your workplace equipment.

28 You've got a plan, now and you're passionately fired up to put it into action. Someone may have doubted you, but will eat their words once they realise what's going on.

29 Today, you could learn some life-shattering lessons about the people with whom you work. Most of them are self-centred but you just hadn't realised that yet. These issues could now be glaring you in the face.

30 An offer may be on the table today, but you find it hard to accept it outright because you realise some other part of your life may have to be sacrificed. Que sera, sera!

OCTOBER

Monthly Highlight

Your level of income might be up, but spending could be punching holes in whatever you earn. Exercise moderation if you want to come out on top.

Unexpected meetings bring pleasure, but also bring tension among your nearest and dearest, who may not approve.

---

1 Your thinking is slow just now, but so it should be. The last thing you want is to rush into a decision that's wrong.

---

2 Build up your energy with plenty of vitamins, minerals and exercise. Of course, don't forget to sleep. If life has been a gruelling journey recently, you'll need the extra energy.

---

3 You need to explore the idea of two souls being as one. With some extra effort, you can direct your partner's attention to investigate these ideas as a couple. Sex should be good at the moment.

---

4 Don't overlook opportunities as a result of unwarranted scepticism. If news arrives, be open to the possibilities before you.

5 Love and passion may fall short of your ideals, and right now you may not be nurtured the way you want. Ask for it.

6 Look at what you are happy about in life rather than focusing on what you don't have. This is how you will attract more positive things into your circle.

7 You may unexpectedly have to deal with someone's misfortune rather than your own work today. You've got more important things to do, but this may take priority.

8 Just let everyday worries pass you by and stop focusing on them. Enjoy your work, and introduce a little fun and laughter to the proceedings. This will make life much more enjoyable.

9 You could struggle with an unexpected decision by a family friend. You may have had your heart set on an event or activity with them, only to find they've let you down. Don't retaliate—not just yet.

10 It's a big step, but now you may be ready to remove some people from your life. With Venus moving away from your zone of friendships, you may realise that it's time to make way for the new.

11 If you prefer to keep things as they've always been, then there'll be no growth, and the friends you have will simply remain the same. Try to do things a little differently, and seek out new acquaintances.

12 There's considerable clarity in your life at present, especially regarding your relationships. You may observe things that help you draw a completely different conclusion, however.

13 It's a case of liking what you happen to be given at the moment. You may have to contend with some disappointment, but did you know that disappointment is often the seed of opportunity?

14 Before you listen to others, have a think about what you want from the situation. A quick phone call or e-mail should clear the air for everyone concerned.

15 Earlier, you may have been certain you didn't want to make a change or move, but now you could be having second thoughts. Look at it this way: it's exciting to consider that changes are coming.

16 Peruse things more carefully before signing on the dotted line, and listen to your partner before giving the nod.

17 You could feel duped by someone, having to pay them more than they're worth. Get some comparative prices before you go out shopping and declaring yourself broke.

18 Pushing and shoving, rushing around madly, and trying to meet unrealistic deadlines could cause you physical injury. Pace yourself.

19 The continuing clash between responsibility and freedom could yield a breakthrough for you today, Libra. You may be surprised to feel that you're more supported than you had first thought. Full steam ahead!

20 Although you want to spend more time alone exploring your own desires and interests, pressing social and family demands won't allow that for a while. Your needs will be at the bottom of the list today.

21 You want to sever ties with someone, but you're conscious of the poor timing. Perhaps it's best to wait for a better moment and forget any grievances you have for a while.

22 Just because you've got concerns over money doesn't mean you should gamble your hard-earned cash away. Very few wealthy people have won it at the horses or the casino.

23 Extravagance and the wild reactions of someone you care for could confuse you today. You're in a state of heightened sensitivity, and high-energy people like this are not conducive to your best interests.

24 Someone who is a nuisance may need to be set straight. Setting boundaries is a theme at the moment, and your discussions could be rather tense.

25 Break down all the barriers between yourself and someone who's remained distant recently. You may need to make an apology for the sake of peace.

26 Cutting off your nose to spite your face is something you'll have to watch today. The best approach is to listen to others, especially if what we're talking about relates to someone in your workplace.

27 Why not take pot luck and accept someone at face value? Time constraints may make it a little difficult to get all the requisite information otherwise. Trust is the key word today.

28 You can expect to make an impressive comeback in an area you previously thought was shut off. A mutual friend will act as the catalyst.

29 Finding a whole new look is important just now if you want to move forward. A change of mind, body and soul seems to be part of the process.

30 Don't have any fear about going for a new job, and be confident you have the skills to satisfy your interviewer. Lots of smiling at the interview will help.

31 There may be problems associated with a new residential situation, and this is because of the way you've structured the loan or your budgets. Rethink all of these things.

❋ NOVEMBER ❋

 Monthly Highlight

This is a lucky month, but don't assume that everything is going to be handed to you on a silver platter. Mars and Jupiter promote your daredevil spirit, but might also make you somewhat inattentive to the finer details.

Be humble, and measure your generosity before offering help and money to others.

1 You are very lucky just now, with the Moon and Jupiter offering you benefits for your past good actions. However, don't waste what comes to you—Mars and Jupiter may make you feel overly confident.

2 Power tripping is part of the game some of your co-workers may play today. Employ the right tactics to deal with people who are ruthless, and put them in their place.

3   You need to look at the true worth of a person you met recently, and don't necessarily assume that helping them is in your best interests. Study their character more thoroughly.

4   Don't give advice today unless it is asked for. If you come across as a know-it-all, it may harm your reputation. You may also want to book a beauty treatment to indulge yourself. You're worth it.

5   You're more passionate about your work at this time, and it's making a great impression on your employers and customers. This is the start of a new professional cycle.

6   Don't give more than you have to, which will require you to investigate another person's needs first. You should also insist that you get your fair share of attention from loved ones today.

7   Your work is getting in the way of a healthy lifestyle. Listen to your friends when they tell you to come along and enjoy a few parties and get-togethers.

8   Progress is something you're going to embrace just now, especially if you realise you've been on the wrong track. Improve what you do and carve out a new pathway for yourself.

9 You could be feeling a little tired—once again, you need to take care of your health and build up your resistance. You're living life in the fast lane now.

10 Is your love life giving you want you want, or are you trying to change your nature to conform to someone else's idea of who you are? Remember, you are you, you don't need to alter anything. You just need to be accepted and accepting.

11 You may need a good friend to listen to your troubles, but by the same token, you are more than happy to listen to them. This is a mutually supportive day.

12 A long walk in fresh air will get you back in touch with your inner spirit. If money troubles are getting the better of you, this is an excellent idea to release the pressure.

13 You have a strong desire to earn more money, but realise you will need to take on additional responsibilities. If you meet these head-on, the forces of karma will be positive, and you'll realise that the extra work is worth the outcome.

14 Usually, it can be a little hard to pierce your armour, but occasionally it's okay to let down your guard and admit you have needs and desires too. Your partner will appreciate your honesty.

15 Praising someone for a job well done will bring satisfaction to you as well as them. You need to show that they are valued, and that it's okay for them to admit their mistakes as well.

16 Someone's telling you that you should work to live, not live to work. Restoring some balance is necessary, so make an appointment with your doctor and dentist to keep up your good health.

17 Someone is trying to manipulate you, and you finally see the pattern. Due to habit, you've always succumbed, but now you may oppose them. This can cause problems.

18 Lighten up! Life doesn't need to be so hard today. Your emotional wellbeing rests upon your ability to relax and be more open to the new people you meet.

19 Your childhood traumas may come to the surface now, and if there are any hang-ups still bothering you, you must deal with them. Get in touch with your inner child.

20 Put your nose to the grindstone and your shoulder to the wheel by all means, but don't go at it too hard. Be wary of taking on more than you can handle today.

21 Compromise is not a word that will sit easily with you right now, but nonetheless, you'll be surprised at the outcome if you give someone else a chance.

22 It's time to begin that new exercise regime you've been promising yourself. The planets indicate that your ideal of who you can be is not in keeping with what you're actually doing. Get fit.

23 Trying out a new hobby or interest with your partner can cement your love life. Try to take interest in what they're doing as well.

24 If you're feeling neglected by others or being criticised unfairly, you may be feeling the pinch. Don't play victim, however, and address the issue in a mature way.

25 You'll be a workaholic just now, but an elevated career path can be yours if you don't give in to the initial hurdles. Venus continues to make you poetic, and a love of music is in the air.

26 Don't let apathy become your tendency. You have the capacity to work hard at the moment, and must utilise determination. Laziness has to be eradicated.

27 A combination of quick learning and an ability with languages, plus a versatile and adaptable nature, makes you an ideal teacher to someone nearby. Helping others with their health and mental states will be a pleasure.

28 Your family will be very important to your wellbeing at the moment. You'll enjoy being with relatives, and someone from the past may also be part of the picture just now.

29 You have vivid and prophetic dreams that may surprise you. Don't be surprised that déjà-vu is revealing insights that you should follow at this time.

30 Your traits of dedication, loyalty and tenacity are holding you in good form. Someone will offer some help that will speed up the process of completing a project today.

✣ DECEMBER ✣

Monthly Highlight

Continuing power plays on the home front make this month another one full of tension. There could be disputes over money or others may be leaning upon you, which could make you feel uncomfortable. Lay down the rules of engagement, reassert your power and take back some control.

---

1 You need to conquer some of your inner fears just now, because a bigger and better position is being offered to you. You may feel as though you can't handle it, but you'll do okay.

---

2 Where are you going in such a hurry? Your lightning-quick, sudden outbursts of anger may be met with ferocity in your workplace. Don't take other people's goodwill for granted.

---

3 Don't throw good money after bad just now, Libra. You are overestimating how much you have. Waste is in the air.

---

4 Society's rules will sometimes strangle you, but with a positive view of life and big plans, you can nurture your progressive mind, and keep your eye on the horizon up ahead. Something new may be presented today.

5 There's some drama behind the scenes, and it's unsettling at the moment. You mustn't buy into idle chit-chat, which just wastes time. Keep your eye on the road and your hands on the wheel.

6 Nobody is liked by everybody, and your erratic behaviour will cause problems in your relationships. Love yourself first, then surround yourself with beautiful people.

7 You may meet someone now who has very similar ideals in life. In fact, you can become great friends. Nurture the relationship.

8 You are magnetic and energetic at present, and this will help you make a great impact on the world with an unconventional approach. Share your ideas with your friends.

9 Your curious nature could prompt you to stumble upon something you hadn't yet realised. This will be useful in your work, and help you earn more money.

MONTHLY PREDICTIONS

10 You must let go of relationships that aren't working. Stand firm and stick to your views. Don't listen to others too much.

11 You must be true to yourself and your heart. You may have an argument with someone today, but know that there may be something below the surface that hasn't yet been spoken of. This will be more to the point.

12 Clouds do have a silver lining, so look for them. There's no crime in being optimistic and ambitious, so get rid of your doubts. Balance brings happiness into your life just now.

13 You'll have to slow your pace today. A fiery temperament will get you into trouble, and if you're in a hurry, you may forget things and make the wrong decisions. Take your time.

14 A friend in need can be a pain today, but there's no way you'll refuse to help. By doing so, you may discover a secret you previously hadn't been aware of.

15 You must tread carefully with a new relationship at present. You are impulsive, and may not have thought things through.

16 Criticism may be hard to take, but as long as it's constructive, it will be exactly what you need to improve yourself. Accept comments with humility.

17 You need to use other people's experience to acquire material possessions. Listening to and learning from someone older and wiser will be useful just now. You may take on a mentor.

18 Unless you carefully direct the powerful energies you are feeling, they will be destructive, particularly for your love life. Master your self-control, and channel it properly to bring happiness.

19 You want to possess beautiful things, but at the moment they could be too expensive for you. If, for example, you want a painting that is beyond your budget, why not paint it yourself?

20 Travelling appeals to you at the moment, but don't run yourself around in circles. Define your objectives, and work towards these goals using your imagination and vision.

21 When I speak of fame, I don't mean world fame, but you have an opportunity to develop a good reputation just now, through your understanding of others and your good service. Enjoy the accolades.

22 Follow your own path, but control your anger and negative emotions—they could make it a lonely course. You should hone your arguing skills in litigation or debates, not in friendships.

23 You could be preoccupied with your own problems just now, and others may regard this as selfish. The element of timing is important so that they feel you're not holding out on them.

24 Your friends may band together to support you as a group during this period. Spontaneous ideas—a think-tank of sorts—will be useful for all involved.

25 Your positive karma is powerful now, and augurs well for your future direction. Knowledge and learning are needed to enhance your destiny.

26 You're being offered some success, but you may have a fear of it. Take control of your energies and know that you're up to the task.

27 Prosperity is a combination of past karma, effort and timing. Use your clever mind and quick wit to be the master of timed moves just now.

28 At present, life will be a tightrope, and even though the Christmas festivities should indicate a break, you may still be working yourself to the bone. Chill out!

29 You must trust in yourself, otherwise you may never trust others. This is the basis of a good relationship. Assure your partner that you are trustworthy.

30 You could feel alone just now, but that's because you've become habituated to having too many people around. Enjoy some silence and a bit of your own space, especially if you have a chance to combine that with nature.

31 The final day of the year is excellent for fulfilling your desires and being in the company of good friends. Enjoy cheerful banter and a cup of coffee while celebrating the end of another year.

2012
ASTRONUMEROLOGY

PREDICTING THE FUTURE IS EASY.
IT'S TRYING TO FIGURE OUT WHAT'S
GOING ON NOW THAT'S HARD.

Fritz R.S. Dressler

THE POWER BEHIND YOUR NAME

It's hard to believe that your name resonates with a numerical vibration, but it's true! Simply by adding together the numbers of your name, you can see which planet rules you and what effects your name will have on your life and destiny. According to the ancient Chaldean system of numerology, each number is assigned a planetary energy, and each alphabetical letter a number, as in the following list:

AIQJY	=	1	Sun
BKR	=	2	Moon
CGLS	=	3	Jupiter
DMT	=	4	Uranus
EHNX	=	5	Mercury
UVW	=	6	Venus
OZ	=	7	Neptune
FP	=	8	Saturn
—	=	9	Mars

Note: The number 9 is not allotted a letter because it was considered 'unknowable'.

Once the numbers have been added, you can establish which single planet rules your name and personal affairs. At this point the number 9 can be used for interpretation. Do you think it's unusual that many famous actors, writers and musicians modify their names? This is to attract luck and good fortune, which can be made easier by using the energies of a friendlier planet. Try experimenting with the table and see how new names affect you. It's so much fun, and you may even attract greater love, wealth and worldly success!

Look at the following example to work out the power of your name. A person named Andrew Brown would calculate his ruling planet by correlating each letter to a number in the table, like this:

A	N	D	R	E	W		B	R	O	W	N
1	5	4	2	5	6		2	2	7	6	5

And then add the numbers like this:

$1 + 5 + 4 + 2 + 5 + 6 + 2 + 2 + 7 + 6 + 5 \quad = \quad 45$

Then add $\quad 4 + 5 \quad = \quad 9$

The ruling number of Andrew Brown's name is 9, which is governed by Mars (see how the 9 can now be used?). Now study the Name-Number Table to reveal the power of your name. The numbers 4 and 5 will play a secondary role in Andrew's character and destiny, so in his case you would also study the effects of Uranus (4) and Mercury (5).

Name Number	Ruling Planet	Name Characteristics
1	Sun	Attractive personality. Magnetic charm. Superman- or superwoman-like vitality and physical energy. Incredibly active and gregarious. Enjoys outdoor activities and sports. Has friends in powerful positions. Good government connections. Intelligent, spectacular, flashy and successful. A loyal number for love and relationships.
2	Moon	Feminine and soft, with an emotional temperament. Fluctuating moods but intuitive, possibly even has clairvoyant abilities. Ingenious nature. Expresses feelings kind-heartedly. Loves family, motherhood and home life. Night owl who probably needs more sleep. Success with the public and/or women generally.

Name Number	Ruling Planet	Name Characteristics
3	Jupiter	A sociable, optimistic number with a fortunate destiny. Attracts opportunities without too much effort. Great sense of timing. Religious or spiritual inclinations. Naturally drawn to investigating the meaning of life. Philosophical insight. Enjoys travel, explores the world and different cultures.
4	Uranus	Volatile character with many peculiar aspects. Likes to experiment and test novel experiences. Forward-thinking, with many extraordinary friends. Gets bored easily so needs plenty of inspiring activities. Pioneering, technological and creative. Wilful and obstinate at times. Unforeseen events in life may be positive or negative.

Name Number	Ruling Planet	Name Characteristics
5	Mercury	Sharp-witted and quick-thinking, with great powers of speech. Extremely active in life: always on the go and living on nervous energy. Has a youthful outlook and never grows old— looks younger than actual age. Has young friends and a humorous disposition. Loves reading and writing. Great communicator.
6	Venus	Delightful and charming personality. Graceful and eye-catching. Cherishes and nourishes friends. Very active social life. Musical or creative interests. Has great money-making opportunities as well as numerous love affairs. A career in the public eye is quite likely. Loves family, but often troubled over divided loyalties with friends.

Name Number	Ruling Planet	Name Characteristics
7	Neptune	Intuitive, spiritual and self-sacrificing nature. Easily duped by those who need help. Loves to dream of life's possibilities. Has healing powers. Dreams are revealing and prophetic. Loves the water and will have many journeys in life. Spiritual aspirations dominate worldly desires.
8	Saturn	Hard-working, ambitious person with slow yet certain achievements. Remarkable concentration and self-sacrifice for a chosen objective. Financially focused, but generous when a person's trust is gained. Proficient in his or her chosen field but a hard taskmaster. Demands perfection and needs to relax and enjoy life more.

Name Number	Ruling Planet	Name Characteristics
9	Mars	Extraordinary physical drive, desires and ambition. Sports and outdoor activities are major keys to health. Confrontational, but likes to work and play really hard. Protects and defends family, friends and territory. Has individual tastes in life, but is also self-absorbed. Needs to listen to others' advice to gain greater success.

YOUR PLANETARY
❖ RULER ❖

Astrology and numerology are intimately connected. Each planet rules over a number between 1 and 9. Both your name and your birth date are governed by planetary energies. As described earlier, here are the planets and their ruling numbers:

1 **Sun**

2 **Moon**

3 **Jupiter**

4 **Uranus**

5 **Mercury**

6 **Venus**

7 **Neptune**

8 **Saturn**

9 **Mars**

To find out which planet will control the coming year for you, simply add the numbers of your birth date and the year in question. An example follows.

If you were born on 14 November, add the numerals 1 and 4 (14, your day of birth) and 1 and 1 (11, your month of birth) to the year in question, in this case 2012 (current year), like this:

Add $1 + 4 + 1 + 1 + 2 + 0 + 1 + 2 \quad = 12$

$$1 + 2 \quad = 3$$

Thus, the planet ruling your individual karma for 2012 would be Jupiter, because this planet rules the number 3.

YOUR PLANETARY
❖ FORECAST ❖

You can even take your ruling name number, as discussed previously, and add it to the year in question to throw more light on your coming personal affairs, like this:

A N D R E W B R O W N	=	9
Year coming	=	2012
Add 9 + 2 + 0 + 1 + 2	=	14
Add 1 + 4	=	5

Thus, this would be the ruling year number based on your name number. Therefore, you would study the influence of Mercury (5) using the Trends for Your Planetary Number table in 2012. Enjoy!

Trends for Your Planetary Number in 2012

Year Number	Ruling Planet	Results Throughout the Coming Year
1	Sun	**Overview**

The commencement of a new cycle: a year full of accomplishments, increased reputation and brand new plans and projects.

Many new responsibilities. Success and strong physical vitality. Health should improve and illnesses will be healed.

If you have ailments, now is the time to improve your physical wellbeing—recovery will be certain.

Love and pleasure

A lucky year for love. Creditable connections with children, family life is in focus. Music, art and creative expression will be fulfilling. New romantic opportunities.

Work

Minimal effort for maximum luck. Extra money and exciting opportunities professionally. Positive new changes result in promotion and pay rises.

Improving your luck

Luck is plentiful throughout the year, but especially in July and August. The 1st, 8th, 15th and 22nd hours of Sundays are lucky.

Lucky numbers are 1, 10, 19 and 28.

Year Number	Ruling Planet	Results Throughout the Coming Year
2	Moon	

Overview

Reconnection with your emotions and past. Excellent for relationships with family members. Moodiness may become a problem. Sleeping patterns will be affected.

Love and pleasure

Home, family life and relationships are focused in 2012. Relationships improve through self-effort and greater communication. Residential changes, renovations and interior decoration bring satisfaction. Increased psychic sensitivity.

Work

Emotional in work. Home career, or hobby from a domestic base, will bring greater income opportunities. Females will be more prominent in your work.

Improving your luck

July will fulfil some of your dreams. Mondays will be lucky: the 1st, 8th, 15th and 22nd hours of them are the most fortunate. Pay special attention to the new and full Moons in 2012.

Lucky numbers include 2, 11, 20, 29 and 38.

Year Number	Ruling Planet	Results Throughout the Coming Year
3	Jupiter	

Overview

A lucky year for you. Exciting opportunities arise to expand horizons. Good fortune financially. Travels and increased popularity. A happy year. Spiritual, humanitarian and self-sacrificial focus. Self-improvement is likely.

Love and pleasure

Speculative in love. May meet someone new to travel with, or travel with your friends and lovers. Gambling results in some wins and some losses. Current relationships will deepen in their closeness.

Work

Fortunate for new opportunities and success. Employers are more accommodating and open to your creative expression. Extra money. Promotions are quite possible.

Improving your luck

Remain realistic, get more sleep and don't expect too much from your efforts. Planning is necessary for better luck. The 1st, 8th, 15th and 24th hours of Thursdays are spiritually very lucky for you.

Lucky numbers this year are 3, 12, 21 and 30. March and December are lucky months. The year 2012 will bring some unexpected surprises.

Year Number	Ruling Planet	Results Throughout the Coming Year
4	Uranus	**Overview**

Overview

Unexpected events, both pleasant and sometimes unpleasant, are likely. Difficult choices appear. Break free of your past and self-imposed limitations. An independent year in which a new path will be forged. Discipline is necessary. Structure your life appropriately, even if doing so is difficult.

Love and pleasure

Guard against dissatisfaction in relationships. Need freedom and experimentation. May meet someone out of the ordinary. Emotional and sexual explorations. Spirituality and community service enhanced. Many new friendships.

Work

Progress is made in work. Technology and other computer or Internet-related industries are fulfilling. Increased knowledge and work skills. New opportunities arise when they are least expected. Excessive work and tension. Learn to relax. Efficiency in time essential. Work with groups and utilise networks to enhance professional prospects.

Year Number	Ruling Planet	Results Throughout the Coming Year

Improving your luck

Moderation is the key word. Be patient and do not rush things. Slow your pace this year, as being impulsive will only lead to errors and missed opportunities. Exercise greater patience in all matters. Steady investments are lucky.

The 1st, 8th, 15th and 20th hours of any Saturday will be very lucky in 2012.

Your lucky numbers are 4, 13, 22 and 31.

Year Number	Ruling Planet	Results Throughout the Coming Year
5	Mercury	

Overview

Intellectual activities and communication increases. Imagination is powerful. Novel and exciting new concepts will bring success and personal satisfaction.

Goal-setting will be difficult. Acquire the correct information before making decisions. Develop concentration and stay away from distracting or negative people.

Love and pleasure

Give as much as you take in relationships. Changes in routine are necessary to keep your love life upbeat and progressive. Develop open-mindedness.

Avoid being critical of your partner. Keep your opinions to yourself. Artistic pursuits and self-improvement are factors in your relationships.

Work

Become a leader in your field in 2012. Contracts, new job offers and other agreements open up new pathways to success. Develop business skills.

Speed, efficiency and capability are your key words this year. Don't be impulsive in making any career changes. Travel is also on the agenda.

Year Number	Ruling Planet	Results Throughout the Coming Year
		Improving your luck
		Write ideas down, research topics more thoroughly, communicate enthusiasm through meetings—this will afford you much more luck. Stick to one idea.
		The 1st, 8th, 15th and 20th hours of Wednesdays are luckiest, so schedule meetings and other important social engagements at these times.
		Throughout 2012 your lucky numbers are 5, 14, 23 and 32.

Year Number	Ruling Planet	Results Throughout the Coming Year
6	Venus	**Overview**

Overview

A year of love. Expect romantic and sensual interludes, and new love affairs. Number 6 is also related to family life. Working with a loved one or family member is possible, with good results. Save money, cut costs. Share success.

Love and pleasure

The key word for 2012 is romance. Current relationships are deepened. New relationships will be formed and may have some karmic significance, especially if single. Spend time grooming and beautifying yourself: put your best foot forward. Engagement and even marriage is possible. Increased social responsibilities. Moderate excessive tendencies.

Work

Further interest in financial matters and future material security. Reduce costs and become frugal. Extra cash is likely. Additional income or bonuses are possible. Working from home may also be of interest. Social activities and work coincide.

Year Number	Ruling Planet	Results Throughout the Coming Year
		Improving your luck

Work and success depend on a creative and positive mental attitude. Eliminate bad habits and personal tendencies that are obstructive. Balance spiritual and financial needs.

The 1st, 8th, 15th and 20th hours on Fridays are extremely lucky this year, and new opportunities can arise when they are least expected.

The numbers 6, 15, 24 and 33 will generally increase your luck.

Year Number	Ruling Planet	Results Throughout the Coming Year
7	Neptune	**Overview**

An intuitive and spiritual year. Your life path becomes clear. Focus on your inner powers to gain a greater understanding and perspective of your true mission in life. Remove emotional baggage. Make peace with past lovers who have hurt or betrayed you. Forgiveness is the key word this year.

Love and pleasure

Spend time loving yourself, not just bending over backwards for others. Sacrifice to those who are worthy. Relationships should be reciprocal. Avoid deception, swindling or other forms of gossip. Affirm what you want in a relationship to your lover. Set high standards.

Work

Unselfish work is the key to success. Learn to say no to demanding employers or co-workers. Remove clutter to make space for bigger and better things. Healing and caring professions may feature strongly. Use your intuition to manoeuvre carefully into new professional directions.

Year Number	Ruling Planet	Results Throughout the Coming Year

Improving your luck

Maintain cohesive lines of communication and stick to one path for best results. Pay attention to health and don't let stress affect a positive outlook. Sleep well, exercise and develop better eating habits to improve energy circulation.

The 1st, 8th, 15th and 20th hours of Wednesdays are luckiest, so schedule meetings and other important social engagements at these times.

Throughout 2012 your lucky numbers are 7, 16, 25 and 34.

Year Number	Ruling Planet	Results Throughout the Coming Year
8	Saturn	

Overview

This is a practical year requiring effort, hard work and a certain amount of solitude for best results. Pay attention to structure, timelines and your diary. Don't try to help too many people, but rather, focus on yourself. This will be a year of discipline and self-analysis. However, income levels will eventually increase.

Love and pleasure

Balance personal affairs with work. Show affection to loved ones through practicality and responsibility.

Dedicate time to family, not just work. Schedule activities outdoors for increased wellbeing and emotional satisfaction.

Work

Money is on the increase this year, but continued focus is necessary. Hard work equals extra income. A cautious and resourceful year, but be generous where possible. Some new responsibilities will bring success. Balance income potential with creative satisfaction.

Year Number	Ruling Planet	Results Throughout the Coming Year

Improving your luck

Being overcautious and reluctant to attempt something new will cause delay and frustration if new opportunities are offered. Be kind to yourself and don't overwork or overdo exercise. Send out positive thought-waves to friends and loved ones. The karmic energy will return.

The 1st, 8th, 15th and 20th hours of Saturdays are the best times for you in 2012.

The numbers 1, 8, 17, 26 and 35 are lucky.

Year Number	Ruling Planet	Results Throughout the Coming Year
9	Mars	

Overview

The ending of one chapter of your life and the preparation for the beginning of a new cycle. A transition period when things may be in turmoil or a state of uncertainty. Remain calm. Do not be impulsive or irritable. Avoid arguments. Calm communication will help find solutions.

Love and pleasure

Tremendous energy and drive help you achieve goals this year. But don't be too pushy when forcing your ideas down other people's throats, so to speak. Diplomatic discussions, rather than arguments, should be used to achieve outcomes. Discuss changes before making decisions with partners and lovers in your life.

Work

A successful year with the expectation of bigger and better things next year. Driven by work objectives or ambition. Tendency to overdo and overwork. Pace your deadlines. Leadership role likely. Respect and honour from your peers and employers.

Year Number	Ruling Planet	Results Throughout the Coming Year

Improving your luck

Find adequate outlets for your high level of energy through meditation, self-reflection and prayer. Collect your energies and focus them on one point. Release tension to maintain health.

The 1st, 8th, 15th and 20th hours of Tuesdays will be lucky for you throughout 2012.

Your lucky numbers are 9, 18, 27 and 36.